The British Inheritance

A TREASURY OF HISTORIC DOCUMENTS

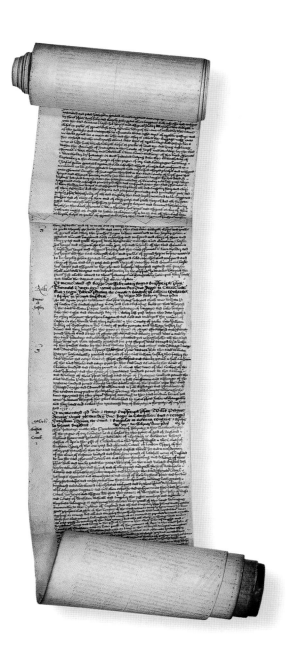

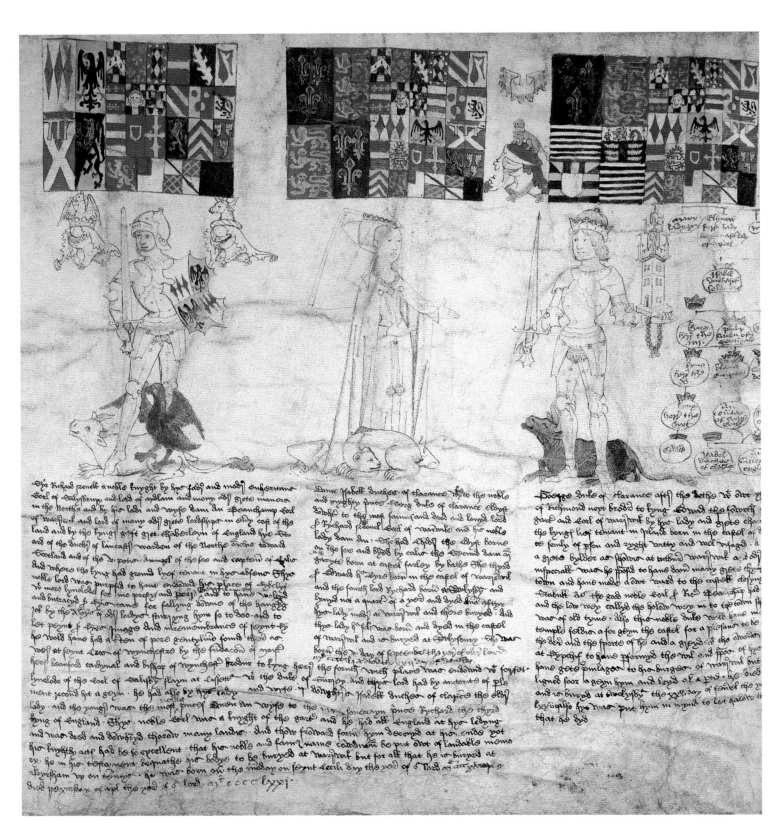

The Rous Roll, an illustrated armorial roll-chronicle by John Rous, chantry priest of Guy's Cliffe in Warwickshire, commemorating benefactors of Warwick and the holders of the Warwick earldom, *c*.1483–85. Shown here are Richard Neville, Earl of Warwick and Salisbury, known as the 'kingmaker' (1428–71); Isabel, wife of George, Duke of Clarence; and George, Duke of Clarence (1449–78).

British Library, Additional MS.48976

The British Inheritance

A TREASURY OF HISTORIC DOCUMENTS

edited by

Elizabeth Hallam and Andrew Prescott

THE BRITISH LIBRARY *and* PUBLIC RECORD OFFICE

Contributors

The British Library
Andrew Prescott

Public Record Office
Elizabeth Hallam Smith
Simon Fowler
Mandy Banton

National Library of Scotland
Iain Gordon Brown
Ian Cunningham
Kenneth Dunn
Louise Yeoman

National Archives of Scotland
Rosemary Gibson
Alison Rosie

National Library of Wales
Dafydd Ifans

Acknowledgements

The editors are grateful to the following for their help: Patrick
Cadell; Paul Carter; Sophie Carter; Olive Geddes; Kathleen
Houghton; Gwyn Jenkins; David Johnson; Paul Johnson; Aidan
Lawes; Rhodri Morgan; Ann Payne; Laurence Pordes; Richard
Price; Angela Roche; Anne Summers; Sarah Tyacke; Anne
Young. Particular thanks to David Way.

Photographic Acknowledgements: British Museum; Fitzwilliam
Museum; House of Lords Record Office; Deidre Grieve; Colin
Hamilton; Sir Paul McCartney; Sony Music.

First published 1999 by
The British Library
96 Euston Road, London NW1 2DB
jointly with the
Public Record Office, Kew, Richmond, Surrey

British Library Cataloguing in Publication Data
A CIP Record for this book is available from The British Library

ISBN 0 7123 4637 6

Designed and typeset by Andrew Shoolbred
Colour origination by South Sea International Press, Hong Kong
Printed and bound in England by
Jarrold Book Printing, Thetford

Contents

Introduction

'We bear witness
West on this windswept Isle'

Orkneyinga Saga, trans. H. Pálsson and P. Edwards

Every autumn, the Henry Wood Promenade Concerts at the Royal Albert Hall in London end with a musical party which is televised all over the world. The Last Night of the Proms, with its traditional patriotic songs such as *Rule Britannia, Jerusalem*, and *Land of Hope and Glory* sung by an audience bedecked in union flags, is one of the most familiar and widely known celebrations of British national feeling. However, a closer examination of the Last Night of the Proms suggests that all is not as it might at first sight seem. The words of the Edwardian *Land of Hope and Glory* became distasteful to Edward Elgar, the composer of the music, after the outbreak of the First World War, and, in the words of *Grove's Dictionary of Music and Musicians*, Elgar 'begged for new, less swaggering words to his tune, but the public was in no mood to learn them'. *Jerusalem*, which since William Blake's words were set to music by Charles Hubert Parry in 1916 has become virtually a second national anthem, is a plea for England to turn its back on those values which in modern times are seen as representing national success, such as industrial and economic prosperity. *Rule Britannia* established itself as a popular song during the rebellion of the Scottish Highlanders in 1745. The national anthem, *God Save the Queen*, likewise became famous when it was sung at the end of theatrical performances at the time when the threat from the Scots was at its greatest in 1745. Some early printings have an extra verse seeking God's help 'Rebellious Scots to crush'.

The Chapter House at Westminster, as reconstructed in the mid-18th century to hold the public records.
Public Record Office, MPB 1/2

There can be few national anthems whose origins can be linked so explicitly with attempts to suppress a substantial part of that nation's population.

Of course, the Last Night of the Proms is primarily an expression of English nationalism, although even this is problematic, since, as George Orwell points out, 'In England all the boasting and flag-waving, the "Rule Britannia" stuff, is done by small minorities. The patriotism of the common people is not vocal or even conscious'. In other words, the Last Night of the Proms is in some ways a very un-English occasion. Wales and Scotland have their own equivalents of the Last Night – a rugby match at Cardiff Arms Park or Burns Night, for example. To the outsider, it may seem surprising that the country which ruled the largest empire the world has ever known should be unsure of its national identity. Nevertheless, as we enter a new millennium, the British sense of identity seems increasingly blurred. The recent rise of national feeling within different parts of the United Kingdom has led some historians to talk of the 'break-up of Britain' or 'unravelling Britain'. It is still too early to say whether the devolution of political power to Wales and Scotland will help stabilise the Union or precipitate its break-up. Such concerns might have seemed strange to a historian writing a hundred years ago at the end of the 19th century, but they would have been familiar at the end of the 18th century, when Anglo-Scottish tensions had loomed very large, or at the end of the 17th century, in which the Union of England and Scotland under a single ruler had helped precipitate a civil war. The present uncertainty about what constitutes British identity is not perhaps the expression of a post-Imperial crisis, but rather a reversion to a normal state of affairs. As Raphael Samuel has put it, 'The unity of the British Isles, so far from being the norm, can appear as an exceptional condition, with a lifespan of less than two hundred years, from the Battle of Culloden, say, in 1746, to the Irish Treaty of 1921.'

Many historians have attempted to pinpoint the key events which contributed to the making of Britain, but the impact and legacy of such events are invariably ambiguous. Roman Britain saw a greater degree of political unity and a larger population than at any time before the 13th century, but it was the arrival of the Anglo-Saxons after the departure of the Romans which gave England its name and language. Anglo-Saxon rulers such as Alfred and Athelstan established a kingdom which was to cover much of England, but there were profound linguistic and cultural divisions, due largely to the extensive Scandinavian settlements in the North and East. The main effect of the Norman Conquest of 1066 was to ensure that English politics became enmeshed with those of France, which in turn helped ensure continuing Scottish independence and limited the impact of English colonisation in Wales. The union of the crowns of England and Scotland under James VI of Scotland and I of England at the beginning of the 17th century did not lead to the 'union of hearts and minds' which James wanted. Indeed, modern interpretations see the conflicts in the reign of James's son Charles as a 'war of the three kingdoms' rather than an 'English Civil War'. The overthrow of the House of Stuart in the 'Glorious Revolution' of 1688, seen by Victorian historians as the formative event in British history, inaugurated a period of tension in Anglo-Scottish relations, which resulted first in the gunshot marriage between England and Scotland in 1707 and then in 1745 in the rebellion of Highlanders loyal to the Stuart pretender 'Bonnie Prince Charlie', in which a Scots invasion reached as far south as Derby and created panic in London, but was eventually ruthlessly suppressed. The aftermath of 1745 was the Highland clearances, in which 'improving' landlords burnt houses over their tenants' heads and offered tenants a choice between immediate emigration to the overseas colonies or gaol.

Viewed through the perspective of the Highland clear-ances, the British Empire appears a less glorious achievement. Indeed, the British Empire, which should perhaps be the defining British achievement, seems in retrospect a ramshackle and odd institution, justly described by Benedict Anderson as a 'grab-bag' which resembled 'those random collections of Old Masters hastily assembled by English and American millionaires which eventually turn into solemnly imperial state museums'. Britain's rise to world economic pre-eminence in the wake of the Industrial Revolution also opened up further fissures, and the 'two nations' question became a major preoccupation, with the split between North and South echoing the divide between urban and rural society and rich and poor. The North-South split in England is found also in Wales, with the divide between the industrial and coal-dependent areas of South Wales against the rural heartlands of the Welsh language to the North, and in Scotland, with the industrial belt in the Lowlands contrasting with the emptying Highlands and their remnants of Gaelic culture.

The familiar events which one might imagine as defining the British inheritance are frequently elusive and difficult to pin down. What seem to provide more substantial landmarks are key texts, whether documents or literature. It might be said that the British inheritance is marked out not so much by events, but by documents whose impact resonates down the ages. The way in which the Norman Conquest turned upside down many aspects of English life is expressed most powerfully in the two monumental volumes of Domesday Book. The grant of liberties in Magna Carta was restricted to only some of the English people, but it established the principle that the power of a king could be limited by a written grant, and came to be regarded as a cornerstone of democracy. The Declaration of Arbroath of 1320 remains one of the most finely-expressed statements of national sovereignty. The way in which the ecclesiastical reforms of the 16th century helped shape national feeling was through the production of texts in the vernacular - bibles, prayerbooks and declarations of faith. Welsh religious dissent was animated by the sermons and hymns of writers like William Williams of Pantycelyn. The Bill of Rights of 1689 remains the nearest thing to a British constitution, and is a fundamental document in the development of the concept of human rights. Part of Britain's legacy to its colonies was the sense of the importance of text as a social and political tool, most famously expressed in the Declaration of Independence. The most powerful font of Britishness is its literature.

English national identity is intimately bound up with the work of writers such as Shakespeare, Austen, Dickens or Orwell. In Scotland, Robert Burns and Walter Scott played vital roles in creating modern Scottish culture, while in Wales the Welsh language and literature, particularly poetry, have been the most fundamental force in maintaining a Welsh national identity.

Visitors to Britain often imagine that the country's great houses, gardens, galleries and museums sum up the British experience. But it is rather through Britain's historical documents and literature that the country's complex and tangled inheritance can best be explored and understood. This book is intended to help present some of that inheritance. It is inevitably extremely partial and selective; the textual heritage of Britain is so rich that it would be impossible to be comprehensive. The selection is limited to Great Britain. The complex story of Ireland's involvement with Britain would have required another book. Sadly, it has also been necessary to omit the more far-flung British Isles, such as the Orkneys and Shetland, only acquired by Scotland from Norway in the 15th century and perhaps still looking more towards Norway than Britain, or the Channel Islands, remnants of the Norman Conquest, where many Anglo-Norman institutions and terminology still survive. Nevertheless, it is hoped that the selection of documents presented here will help convey how words and texts have helped shape Britain.

Given the significance of texts in the British inheritance, it is not surprising that the places which store these texts have become major emblems of British national identity. The two most important repositories of historical documents in England are the Public Record Office and The British Library, although the significance of local life in England is reflected in the way in which local archives, themselves of great value, are stored in a network of county record offices. The British Library was formed in 1973 from the amalgamation of a number of national library services, including the British Museum Library, which contained the national collection of private manuscripts and documents. The manuscript collections of the British Library were moved from the British Museum building to the Library's new premises at St Pancras in 1998. The British Museum is of course one of the most famous British institutions; a former director of the Museum, Sir Frederick Kenyon, wrote in 1946 that 'The British Museum is, next to the British Navy, the national institution which is held in the most universal respect abroad'. The core of its manuscript collections were the medieval monastic records saved by 16th- and 17th-century antiquaries such as Sir Robert Cotton following the dissolution of the monasteries. As new manuscripts were acquired by the Museum in the 18th and 19th centuries, they inevitably reflected the view of history and Britain's place in the world held by the officials in charge, and, as Kenyon's comment suggests, the holdings very much tell an imperial story - indeed, in some respects the manuscript collections are almost an imperial mausoleum. Heroes of the British Empire feature prominently from, Francis Drake to Captain Cook, Nelson, Wellington, Florence Nightingale, General Gordon, Captain Scott and General Haig (although there are also some unexpected figures there, such as the social reformers Francis Place and Marie Stopes).

While The British Library is a repository of private papers, the Public Record Office contains the records of government. Victorian historians saw the British constitution as the product of organic development over many centuries uninterrupted by invasion or revolution, and the public records seem a powerful symbol of such a view. They begin with Domesday Book. The oldest record classes begin in the 12th century and continue in unbroken sequence to modern times. In 1998, the records filled over 167 kilometres of shelving, literally millions of papers, parchment rolls, maps, plans and photographs – even objects as varied as medieval coin dies and samples of 19th-century buttons. These archives have been held in various locations including the Tower of London and Westminster Abbey, but after the foundation of the Public Record Office in 1838 they were consolidated in a specially designed building on a site in Chancery Lane which had itself been used for storage of records since the 14th century. One of the custodians of the records referred to this huge fire-proof repository as 'the strong box of the Empire'. The records outgrew the Chancery Lane accommodation and in 1977 a new state-of-the-art office was opened in the West London suburb of Kew. In 1996, the remaining records at Chancery Lane were removed to Kew, and, although the historic censuses are still available on microfilm in central London, the great bulk of the oldest and most complete national archive in the world is now once more together under one roof.

In Wales and Scotland, archives and libraries have been intimately linked with ideas of national identity. The records of Scotland were kept from the earliest times at Edinburgh Castle, but suffered major losses when documents were removed by Edward I and Oliver Cromwell. The loss of these records, it was noted, 'deprived Scotland of something essential to its character and personality', and this was recognised in the Articles of Union in 1707 which declared that the Scottish public records should 'continue to be kept as they are within that part of the United Kingdom now called Scotland, and that they shall so remain in all time coming'. The archives had by this time been moved to the Scottish parliament house, but conditions there were extremely unsatisfactory, and work on a new Register House in Edinburgh's New Town began in 1774. The Register House developed into a fully-fledged national record collection during the 19th century and acts of 1937 and 1948 put the Scottish Record Office – now renamed as the National Archives of Scotland – on a statutory footing. The National Library of Scotland owes its origins to Scotland's separate legal system. It was founded over 300 years ago as the Library of the Faculty of Advocates. In 1710 the Copyright Act of Queen Anne gave the Library the right to obtain a copy of every book published in Great Britain, a privilege retained by the Library to this day. The Advocates' Library had by the end of the 19th century developed into a national library in all but name, but the upkeep of the library proved too great a burden for a private body, and the Faculty presented its collections to the nation, allowing the formal establishment in 1925 of the National Library of Scotland.

From 1880-81 there was a great upsurge of national feeling in Wales, expressed primarily in the enormous growth in chapel membership and in the popularity of the reorganised *eisteddfod* with its grand finale of the male voice choir competition. There was a vigorous campaign for the disestablishment of the Welsh Church, in recognition of the overwhelmingly non-conformist religious allegiance of the Welsh. A federal University of Wales was established in 1896, and attempts were made to create a separate Welsh board of education. The Welsh Office was established in 1907. Two years previously, governmental permission was given for the establishment of a National Library of Wales at Aberystwyth. The choice of this small seaside town for the site of the national library was due to the fact that Lord Rendel had donated land for it there and also that the manuscript collector Sir John Williams had made the gift of his remarkable collection of manuscripts conditional on the Library being founded at Aberystwyth. The first national librarian, John Ballinger, formerly head of the free library at Cardiff, rapidly established the new Library as a centre of Welsh historical and literary studies, and a major force in the continued revival of the Welsh language and culture in the 20th century.

These different archives and libraries are deeply connected with the different national aspirations of the peoples who inhabit Great Britain. An image common to all these institutions is that they see themselves as the treasure houses of the various nations which they serve. This book aims to provide a quick look into the vast treasuries of these different island peoples.

The Middle Ages

King of the perennial holly-groves, the riven sandstone: overlord of the M5: architect of the historic rampart and ditch, the citadel at Tamworth, the summer hermitage in Holy Cross: guardian of the Welsh Bridge and the Iron Bridge: contractor to the desirable new estates: saltmaster: moneychanger: commissioner for oaths: martyrologist: the friend of Charlemagne.

'I liked that', said Offa, 'sing it again'.

Geoffrey Hill, *Mercian Hymns*

The Roman Empire in Britain crumbled away in the late 4th century. As successive candidates for the imperial title sought military support and the Empire found its overextended boundaries under attack at many points, Britain was gradually denuded of Roman troops. The Emperor advised the British population to make its own defence arrangements. German mercenaries were used, but they rebelled against their employers and became the vanguard of large-scale Germanic immigration. Despite British resistance led by Arthur and others, much of England fell under the political domination of three groups, the Angles, the Saxons and the Jutes.

Britain dissolved into tiny statelets. These coalesced into larger regional units such as Mercia in the Midlands of England and Northumbria in the North. The memory of these Anglo-Saxon kingdoms and their rulers still haunts many of the English regions; the modern poet Geoffrey Hill has depicted the 8th-century Mercian king Offa, who built an immense dyke to mark the boundary between his kingdom and those of the Welsh princes, as the presiding spirit of the West Midlands of England.

From the late 8th century, all of Britain was subject to Viking attack. In Wales, the impact was limited to the coast, but England and Scotland were transformed. All the ancient English kingdoms were overrun except Wessex and there was extensive Scandinavian settlement in the North and East. In Scotland, the northern and western isles became Viking colonies, and the Viking attacks gave a strong impetus to political union. The Scandinavian orientation of Britain by the early 11th century is apparent from the incorporation of England in the 'North Sea Empire' of Cnut ('King Canute').

The departure of the Romans, as envisaged by a 13th-century artist.
British Library, Egerton MS. 3028, f.12

In 1066, England faced two invasions: the first, unsuccessful, from Norway; the second, successful, by William, Duke of Normandy, itself an area of Viking settlement (the Normans were literally 'Northmen', men originally from the North). Under William's successors, England became part of an empire covering much of northern and western France. The English kings became preoccupied with their French possessions and were less concerned with extending their power on the British mainland. Although Wales was conquered at the end of the 13th century, English authority there remained fitful away from the borders and coastal margins. Norman interventions in the North encouraged the development of a united and strong Scottish monarchy, and Scotland successfully resisted English attempts to swallow it up.

Even after the English kings had lost most of their French possessions in the 13th century, they hankered after the title of King of France and engaged in a 'Hundred Years War' to pursue their continental dreams. Noted triumphs by the English at Crécy in 1346, where victory was due largely to the contingent of over 5,000 Welsh soldiers in their distinctive national uniform of green and white, and Agincourt in 1415, where Welsh soldiers also played an important part, did not however lead to any permanent domination over parts of France. The defeat of Richard III in 1485 by the Welshman Henry Tudor, who became Henry VII, has been taken as marking the end of the middle ages in Britain, but perhaps more significant landmarks were the cession of Orkney and Shetland by Norway to Scotland in 1472 and the loss of Calais, England's last French dominion, in 1558.

King Arthur is one of the most famous figures in British history, but is also one of the most mysterious. All that is known is that he was a warrior who led native British forces against Saxon invaders sometime after the final departure of the Roman legions. By the early 12th century, the legend of Arthur as an ideal king with his idyllic court at Camelot was firmly established in Wales, Cornwall and Brittany, and the inhabitants of those regions dreamed that he would eventually return to drive out the English. The 12th-century writer Geoffrey of Monmouth gave the legend of Arthur wider currency, presenting him as the perfect Christian king, so that English kings, beginning with Richard I, began to present themselves as the successors of Arthur. The cult of Arthur has remained potent until modern times, so that the poet Tennyson declared that Prince Albert, Queen Victoria's husband, would find in Arthur 'some image of himself'.

Geoffrey of Monmouth's legendary history of Britain was popularised by a poet called Wace, who in about 1155 produced a French poem called *Brut*, after Brutus, the supposed founder of Britain, which drew heavily on Geoffrey's work. The legend of the round table makes its first appearance in Wace. This illustration of Arthur's coronation is taken from a 13th-century copy of *Brut*.
British Library, Egerton MS. 3028, f. 37

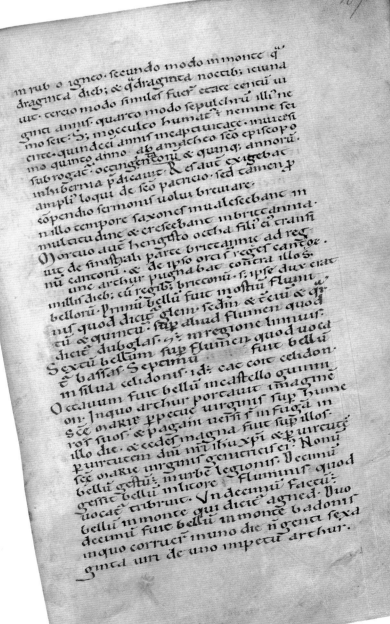

'The History of the Britons' is one of the few surviving accounts of events after the departure of the Romans. It has been attributed to Nennius, a Welsh monk who lived at the beginning of the 9th century. It contains one of the earliest references to Arthur, listing twelve battles fought by him and stating that he was 'victorious in all his campaigns'. This is the oldest known manuscript of Nennius, and dates from the 10th century.
British Library, Harley MS. 3859, f. 187

Alfred 'the Great'

King Alfred (849–899) was the most remarkable of the Anglo-Saxon kings. Many legends grew up about him, some encouraged by Alfred himself, which became important components of the English national myth. Alfred's childhood was overshadowed by the threat of Viking attack. He succeeded his brother Æthelred as King of Wessex in 871, shortly after they had both managed to inflict a defeat on the Viking army at Ashdown in Berkshire. Alfred's initial attempts to resist the Vikings were unsuccessful, and by 878 he had taken refuge in a remote fortress at Athelney in Somerset. He sent secret messages to his army to meet him at a place called Egbert's Stone and inflicted a devastating defeat on the Vikings at Edington in Wiltshire. Alfred's recovery from his low ebb at Athelney may be seen as the first expression of a key motif in the English national myth, the underdog successfully fighting back against impossible odds. By 886, Alfred had captured the city of London and he began to style himself King of the Anglo-Saxons. Although he only directly ruled part of southern England, Alfred was perhaps the first ruler to think of himself as the leader of all English people. The innovative measures taken by him to reorganise his kingdom's defences enabled him successfully to resist further Viking attacks from 893 onwards. Alfred was concerned to repair the cultural damage caused by the Viking assaults on churches and monasteries, and encouraged the translation into English of key religious and philosophical texts. It is characteristic of the way tales collected around Alfred that the most famous story about him, of his burning the cakes during his time at Athelney, is probably a 12th-century invention.

Portrait of Alfred from a 14th-century copy of his laws.
British Library, Cotton MS. Claudius D. ii, f. 8

The Anglo-Saxon Chronicle is the oldest history of a European people in their own language. It was initially compiled in about 890-2 by a team of annalists who, even if they were not part of Alfred's immediate circle, were clearly inspired by his cultural programme and were anxious to glorify the Wessex royal dynasty. The core text was distributed to various monasteries, where the monks kept it up to date, adding their own annals for each year. Seven different manuscripts survive. This passage comes from the 'D' text, which was copied out in the mid-11th century. The annal shown here records the victory of Aethelred and Alfred at Ashdown in 871: *In this year the [Viking] army came to Reading in Wessex, and, three nights after, two jarls rode up when the earl Ethelwulf met them at Inglefield and there fought against them and gained the victory; and one of them was there slain, whose name was Sidroc. Four nights after this king Aethelred and Alfred his brother led a large force to Reading and fought against the army, and there was great slaughter made on each side; and earl Athelwulf was slain, and the Danes held possession of the battleplace. And four nights after, King Aethelred and Alfred his brother fought with all the army at Ashdown.*
British Library, Cotton MS. Tiberius B. iv, ff. 33v-34

The records of the English government and state stretch back over more than 900 years to Domesday Book, England's first and most remarkable public record, which is even today legally admissable evidence on title to land. Domesday's coverage of places and people was unmatched in its scope and detail until the very different census returns of the 19th century; and its popular myth as an all-encompassing, authoritative record against which there can be no appeal and equating it with the Day of Judgement, emerged soon after its creation and still endures.

Compiled between 1086 and about 1090, Domesday Book is a magisterial and detailed title deed of the Norman Conquest in 1066, combining legal, feudal and fiscal information. It is at once the product of the sophisticated administration developed over the previous 300 years by the Anglo-Saxon kings of England, and a manifestation of the ruthless determination of William the Conqueror, one of the most brutally effective monarchs ever to have ruled England.

At his Christmas court in 1085 William, says one contemporary, 'had much thought and very deep discussion about this country – how it was occupied and what sorts of people'. As a result, relates another, 'he made a survey of all of England; of the lands in each of the counties; of the possessions of each of the magnates, their lands, their men both bond and free, of the services and payments from each and every estate'. To do this he divided England into areas (probably seven) and sent round commissioners to take and record sworn evidence at the local courts. 'After these investigators came others who were sent to unfamiliar counties to check the first description and to denounce wrongdoers to the king'. This stage of the survey was completed probably by August 1086.

The returns were next collated and gathered together where they were digested and carefully summarised into their final form of Domesday Book. Little Domesday, long thought of as a final draft of the returns for Essex, Norfolk and Suffolk, is the earlier volume and was the work of many scribes; Great Domesday, which covers the whole of the rest of the country, was substantially written by one person, a remarkable achievement. Together the two volumes, now bound up in five parts, cover 37 pre-1974 English counties including the Welsh borders, but excluding Durham, Northumberland, London and Winchester. Domesday's total of 888 parchment folios contain some two million words, in abbreviated Latin, and name 13,418 places, the majority of which still exist as settlements.

For its first five centuries Domesday Book remained primarily a working document – albeit one treated with exceptional reverence and care. From the 16th century its keepers at the Treasury of Receipt at Westminster opened it up

A 15th-century drawing of William the Conqueror surrounded by his followers, presenting a charter to Count Alan of Brittany, from the Register of the Honour of Richmond.
BL Cotton MS Faustina B. vii, f. 72v

Domesday Book

increasingly to scholars and antiquarians, who became its main users – and by 1859, when it was moved to the Public Record Office, Chancery Lane, the manuscript had acquired the iconic significance which it still has today.

Although peasants living on royal lands were later to look back to Domesday for proof of special rights and privileges, contemporaries held the survey in fear and awe for its depth and thoroughness – and in the intervening centuries it has often been presented as a symbol of Norman oppression. But its special significance has never been lost sight of, and today it is regarded as one of England's great national treasures.

Essex
Land of Geoffrey de Mandeville
Hundred of Lexden

Geoffrey holds Marks Tey in demesne [lordship], which Wulfric held in the time of King Edward [1066] as a manor, for 1 1/2 hides [a hide was about 120 acres] and 20 acres. Then 11 bordars [unfree peasants], now 15. Always 4 slaves and 2 ploughs in demesne. Then among the men 4 ploughs, now 2 1/2. Wood for 100 pigs and 20 acres of meadow. Then Geoffrey acquired 250 sheep, 8 cattle, 6 calves, 2 cobs, 28 pigs, 2 beehives. Now [there are] 67 sheep, 4 cattle, 6 calves, 2 cobs and 21 pigs. In the same place 20 sokemen [free in person but with ties to the land] held 1 1/2 hides and 20 acres. Now 30 sokemen hold that land and they cannot withdraw from that manor. They have always had 3 ploughs [and] six acres of meadow. Then and when received [by Geoffrey] it was worth £7; now £10.

Extract from Little Domesday giving the entry for Marks Tey, Essex. This shows that the manor, part of the lands of Earl Geoffrey de Mandeville, one of William the Conqueror's barons, had in 1066 belonged to an Anglo-Saxon, Wulfric. The entry gives information about livestock as well as the land and people, and is characteristic of the greater detail in Little Domesday. An Essex village of 900 years ago is brought vividly to life.
PRO E 31/1/1, f. 57v

- In the time of King EDWARD THE CITY of Leicester rendered to the king £30 a year by tale at 20[d.] to the ora and 15 sesters of honey.

- When the king went with his army by land 12 burgesses from this borough went with him. If, however, he went against an enemy by sea they sent him 4 horses from the same borough as far as London to carry weapons or other things of which there might be need.

- King William now has £42. 10s. by weight for all the rents of the same city and shire. For a hawk, £10 by tale. For a sumpter horse, 20s. From the moneyers, £20 a year at 20[d.] to the ora. Of these £20 Hugh de Grandmesnil has the third penny.

- The king has in LEICESTER 39 houses.

The Archbishop of York, 2 houses with sake and soke and pertaining to Tur Langton.

Earl Hugh, 10 houses which pertain to Barrow upon Soar and 6 houses pertaining to Kegworth and 1 house pertaining to Loughborough.

The Abbey of Coventry has 10 houses.

The Abbey of Crowland has 3 houses. From all these the king has his geld.

Hugh de Grandmesnil has 110 houses and 2 churches.

Besides these he has 24 houses in common with the king in the same borough.

Besides these the same Hugh has in Leicester 24 burgesses pertaining to Anstey and 13 burgesses pertaining to Sileby and 3 houses pertaining to Ingarsby and 10 houses pertaining to Belgrave and 4 houses pertaining to Broughton Astley and 9 houses pertaining to Stockerston and 4 houses pertaining to Wigston Magna and 7 houses pertaining to Enderby and 3 houses pertaining to Earl Shilton and 10 houses pertaining to Birstall and 3 houses pertaining to Burton Overy and 1 house pertaining to 'Bromkinsthorpe' [in St Mary, Leicester] and 2 houses pertaining to Desford and 3 houses pertaining to "Legham", which he bought of Osbern, and 1 house pertaining to "Letitone" and 1 house pertaining to Thurcaston.

In the same borough the same Hugh has 2 churches, and 2 houses and 4 waste houses.

Hugh de Gouville holds 5 houses of Hugh himself with sake and soke. These are in exchange for Watford [Northants].

Robert de Vessey has 6 houses with sake and soke pertaining to Newton Harcourt, and 3 others with sake and soke pertaining to Kibworth Harcourt.

Geoffrey de la Guerche [has] 1 house pertaining to Little Dalby and another pertaining to Pickwell.

☒   In Leicester are 4 houses pertaining to Shepshed and 1 pertaining to Saddington and 1 pertaining to Thorpe Acre.

In this borough Henry de Ferrers and Robert Despenser has [sic] 1 burgess.

Countess JUDITH has 28 houses in the same borough, and 5s. 4d. from half a mill. Outside the borough she herself has 6 carucates of land belonging to the borough, and has there 1 plough, and her men [have] 3 ploughs. There are 8 acres of meadow, [and] woodland 6 furlongs long and 3 furlongs broad. The whole is worth 40s.

The woodland of the whole sheriffdom is called "HERESWODE". It is †4† leagues in length and 1 league in breadth.

HERE ARE ENTERED THE HOLDERS OF LANDS IN LEICESTERSHIRE

- I KING WILLIAM
II The Archbishop of York
III The Bishop of Lincoln
IIII The Bishop of Coutances
V The Abbey of Peterborough
VI The Abbey of Coventry
VII The Abbey of Crowland
VIII Godwine the priest and other almsmen
IX The Count of Meulan
X Earl Aubrey
XI Countess Godgifu
XII Countess Ælfgifu
XIII Earl Hugh
XIIII Hugh de Grandmesnil
XV Henry de Ferrers
XVI Robert de Tosny
XVII Robert de Vessey
XVIII Roger de Bully
XIX Robert Despenser
XX Robert the usher
XXI Ralph de Mortimer
XXII Ralph fitzHubert

XXIII Guy de Raimbeaucourt
XXIIII Guy de Craon
XXV William Peverel
XXVI William Bonvalet
XXVII William Lovet
XXVIII Geoffrey Alselin
XXIX Geoffrey de la Guerche
XXX Godfrey de Cambrai
XXXI Gunfrid de Chocques
XXXII Humphrey the chamberlain
XXXIII Gilbert de Ghent
XXXIIII Gerbert
XXXV Durand Malet
XXXVI Drogo de la Beuvriere
XXXVII Mainou the Breton
XXXVIII Ogier the Breton
XXXIX Nigel d'Aubigny
XL Countess Judith
XLI Adeliza wife of Hugh
XLII Herbert and other sergeants of the king   Earl
XLIII Hugh
XLIIII The men of the Count of Meulan

THE LAND OF THE KING

IN FRAMLAND WAPENTAKE

- The king holds CROXTON KERRIAL. There are 24 carucates of land. In demesne are 2 ploughs and 5 slaves; and 22 villans with 2 bordars have 2½ ploughs, and 30 sokemen have 8 ploughs. There are 30 acres of meadow, and 2 mills rendering 8s.

To this manor pertains KNIPTON. There are 8 carucates of land and 6 bovates. In demesne are 2 ploughs and 4 slaves; and 10 villans with 4 bordars and 10 sokemen have 4 ploughs. There are 6 mills rendering 13s. 4d., and 13 acres of meadow.

To the same manor pertains HARSTON. There are 12 carucates of land. There 20 sokemen with 5 villans and 1 bordar have 6½ ploughs. There are 17 acres of meadow. The whole was worth £10; now £17.

- The king holds NETHER BROUGHTON. There are 12 carucates of land. In demesne is 1 plough; and 24 sokemen with 9 villans and 4 bordars have 12 ploughs. There are 100 acres of meadow. It was worth £3; now £8. Earl Morcar held these 2 manors. Now Hugh fitzBaldric holds them at farm of the king.

- The king holds ROTHLEY. King Edward held it. There are 5 carucates of land. In demesne are 2 of these and there are 2 ploughs; and 29 villans with a priest and 18 bordars have 6 ploughs. There is a mill rendering 4s., and 37 acres of meadow. [There is] demesne woodland 1 league long and half a league broad, [and] woodland of the villans 4 furlongs long and 3 furlongs broad. This vill is worth 62s. a year.

To this manor belong the following members:

First folio of the Great Domesday description of Leicestershire showing the entry for the borough of Leicester, the list of landholders in the county, then the first three entries in the first section, the lands of the king. The manorial entries are written in a highly abbreviated Latin in a formulaic and far more summary form than in Little Domesday, but the borough entries, as here, often provide a great deal of detail. The script is Caroline minuscule with key headings written or scored through in red so that they stand out (the technique is known as rubrication).

PRO E 31/2/2, f. 230r
(Translation reproduced by courtesy of Alecto Historical Editions)

Domesday Book

Thomas Becket (c. 1120–1170) was the focus of the most important national cult of medieval England. He was the son of a prosperous London merchant, who became a clerk of the Archbishop of Canterbury, Theobald of Bec. At Theobald's recommendation, Thomas was appointed Chancellor of England by Henry II. Thomas was a loyal servant to Henry, and became a favourite of the king. When Archbishop Theobald died, Henry was determined that Thomas should be his successor, and on 2 June 1162 Thomas was consecrated as Archbishop of Canterbury. To Henry's astonishment, Thomas gave immediate notice that he intended to put the interests of the church first by resigning the chancellorship. In 1164, Thomas opposed Henry's attempts to restrict the legal immunities of the clergy, and he was forced to flee the country. Under the threat of papal sanctions, Henry agreed to a reconciliation, and Thomas returned to England in November 1170. Alleging, however, that the king had failed to keep his word, and having excommunicated some royal supporters, Thomas appealed to the pope. This infuriated Henry, who in his rage berated his retinue for failing to deal with this low-born clerk. Four knights took Henry at his word, and left for Canterbury. On 29 December 1170, they murdered Thomas at Canterbury Cathedral. Thomas was immediately acclaimed as a martyr, and miracles were reported at his tomb. He was canonised in 1173. The pilgrimage to his shrine at Canterbury was one of the most important expressions of popular devotion in the middle ages, but at the time of the Reformation Henry VIII declared Becket a traitor and eradicated his cult.

Only one example of the various seals which were used by Thomas to authenticate documents in his different official capacities has survived. This is a personal seal, used by him shortly after he was appointed royal Chancellor in 1155. The seal had probably been acquired by him while he was still in Archbishop Theobald's household. It has the legend 'Sigillum Tome Lund' (the seal of Thomas of London). The matrix used to make the seal impression incorporated an ancient gem, which shows a naked, helmeted figure, perhaps Mercury, resting against a pillar.
Public Record Office, E40/4913

Becket was a skilful propagandist, and copies of his letters were widely circulated. A massive collection of Becket's letters was prepared by Alan, Prior of Canterbury and afterwards Abbot of Tewkesbury. This representation of Becket's martyrdom occurs at the beginning of Alan's own working copy of his collection of the Becket correspondence. The miniature shows, in the top half, the arrival of the knights, then, bottom left, Reginald fitz-Urse striking the first blow, and finally, bottom right, the murderers doing penance at Becket's tomb. This is apparently the earliest representation of the martyrdom, dating from about 1171.
British Library, Cotton MS. Claudius B. ii, f. 341

The Exchequer and Taxation

Founded in about 1110 during the reign of King Henry I, the Exchequer was England's earliest government department; and although from the 17th century it gradually lost ground to the Treasury and was finally abolished in 1833 it lives on in the title of Britain's minister of Finance: the Chancellor of the Exchequer. Its name – *eschequier* in French, *scaccarium* in Latin – came from the great chequered cloth, an abacus on which the sums of money owed to the king from various sources were computed, using counters. Through its doors at Westminster came twice a year the sheriffs, the king's officials in the counties, to bring and account for the money they had collected for their sovereign and expended on his behalf.

Tallies were used at the Lower Exchequer (or Exchequer of Receipt) up to 1826 as a record of payment of moneys. They were made from strips of wood into which notches were cut to signify the amount paid — also written on both sides. The stick was then split lengthways and one section was kept by the person paying, the other by the Crown. Examples such as these medieval tallies are a rarity, since most were destroyed by a wholesale burning in 1834 which took most of the Houses of Parliament with it.
Public Record Office, E 402/347

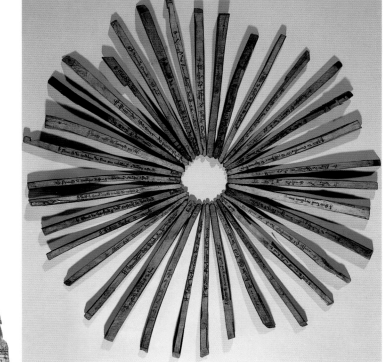

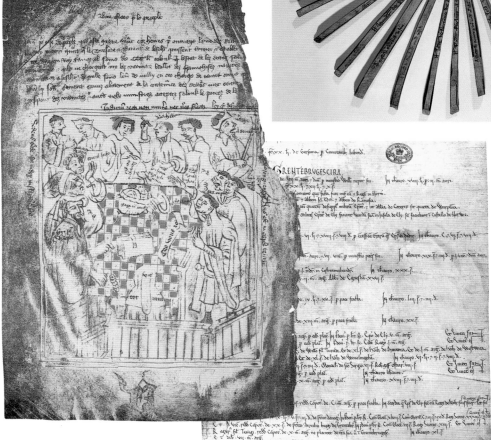

(far left) The sheriffs' accounts were audited in the Upper Exchequer by the Chancellor and Barons of the Exchequer. Although the process might appear like a game of chess, its purpose was very serious: severe penalties were exacted for defrauding the King. This valuable depiction of the Exchequer in action is from a Victorian facsimile of a 15th-century Irish manuscript, now lost.
Facsimiles of Irish Manuscripts, III, plate xxxvii

(left) Finally the sheriffs' accounts were written up onto the Pipe Rolls, which were formed of pieces of parchment joined into strips and sewn at the top. The name of the rolls probably derives from the resemblance of the membranes, when rolled up, to a pipe. This is the entry for Cambridgeshire from the 1129 roll, the first to survive; their format remained the same until they were discontinued in 1833.
Public Record Office, E 372/1, m. 9

The Welsh king Hywel Dda ('Hywel the Good') died in 949 or 950, having ruled peaceably over as great a part of Wales as any ruler before or after. His name is indelibly connected with the work of reforming and creating uniformity in Welsh law. The earliest surviving manuscript of the laws associated with Hywel's name, apparently first written down during his reign, dates from the second quarter of the 13th century. Most of the surviving manuscripts originated in Gwynedd, the homeland of the dominant Welsh rulers of the last hundred years of Welsh independence. They are small, well-used, practical books, carried around by lawyers, rather than intended for libraries. This manuscript, in the National Library of Wales, is one of this first generation of lawbooks and is unique in that it contains a series of illustrations highlighting points discussed in the text.

National Library of Wales, Peniarth MS. 28, f. 1v

Gerald de Barri (*c.* 1146–1223), known often as Gerald of Wales, was one of the most lively and entertaining medieval Latin writers. In books such as his *Topography of Ireland, Journey through Wales and Description of Wales*, he helped pioneer ethnographic writing, and his works are fundamental sources for understanding medieval Welsh and Irish society. Gerald was of both Welsh and Norman extraction, and his outlook reflected the intricacies of noble society in 12th-century south Wales, so that he sometimes sided with the Welsh against the Normans and vice versa. Educated at Gloucester and Paris, Gerald was twice nominated as Bishop of St Davids, only to be rejected by Henry II and the archbishop of Canterbury. Gerald travelled far and wide, including three visits to the pope in Rome. This manuscript of Gerald's *Topography of Ireland* is illustrated with marginal drawings of some of the legends and curiosities described by Gerald. The illustrations (left and below) are perhaps derived from drawings by Gerald himself. Shown here are sketches of an Irish harp-player and the men of Connaught in a coracle.

British Library, Royal MS. 13 B.VIII, ff. 26, 29

Celtic Heroes

Llywelyn ap Iorwerth (1173–1240) was the most powerful ruler Wales had yet seen, and within a short time of his death became known as 'The Great'. By 1208, he had established himself as the ruler of Gwynedd, southern Powys and Ceredigion. His success in resisting King John's attempt to conquer Wales made him by far the most prestigious Welsh ruler, and during the English civil war that followed the grant of Magna Carta, he pushed his authority as far south as Swansea. A cornerstone of Llywelyn's policy was his alliance with Ranulph, Earl of Chester, which was cemented by this marriage settlement agreed on the occasion of the marriage of Llewelyn's daughter Helen to Ranulf's heir, his nephew John.

British Library, Cotton Ch. xxiv.17

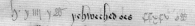

Regarded as Prince of Wales and a national hero, Owain Glyndŵr (*c.* 1354–1416) is remembered for his rebellion against the forces of Henry IV at the beginning of the 15th century. An attack at Rhuthun in 1400 was followed by a victory over royal forces in the Pumlumon hills in the summer of 1401. Glyndŵr captured Aberystwyth and Harlech castles in 1404 and held a parliament at Machynlleth. His aspirations for Wales included the establishment of an independent Welsh Church and the creation of two Welsh universities. Following a defeat in May 1405 his influence subsided but he held out for many years in the mountains of central Wales. After 1412 he is not heard of any more, but lived until 1416, possibly at the home of his daughter Alice Scudamore in Herefordshire. Shown here is part of the 16th-century Welsh chronicle of Ellis Gruffydd describing a meeting between Glyndŵr and the Abbot of Valle Crucis, in which the Abbot declared to Glyndŵr that he had 'arisen a hundred years too early'.

National Library of Wales, NLW MS 3054 (Mostyn 158), f. 285v

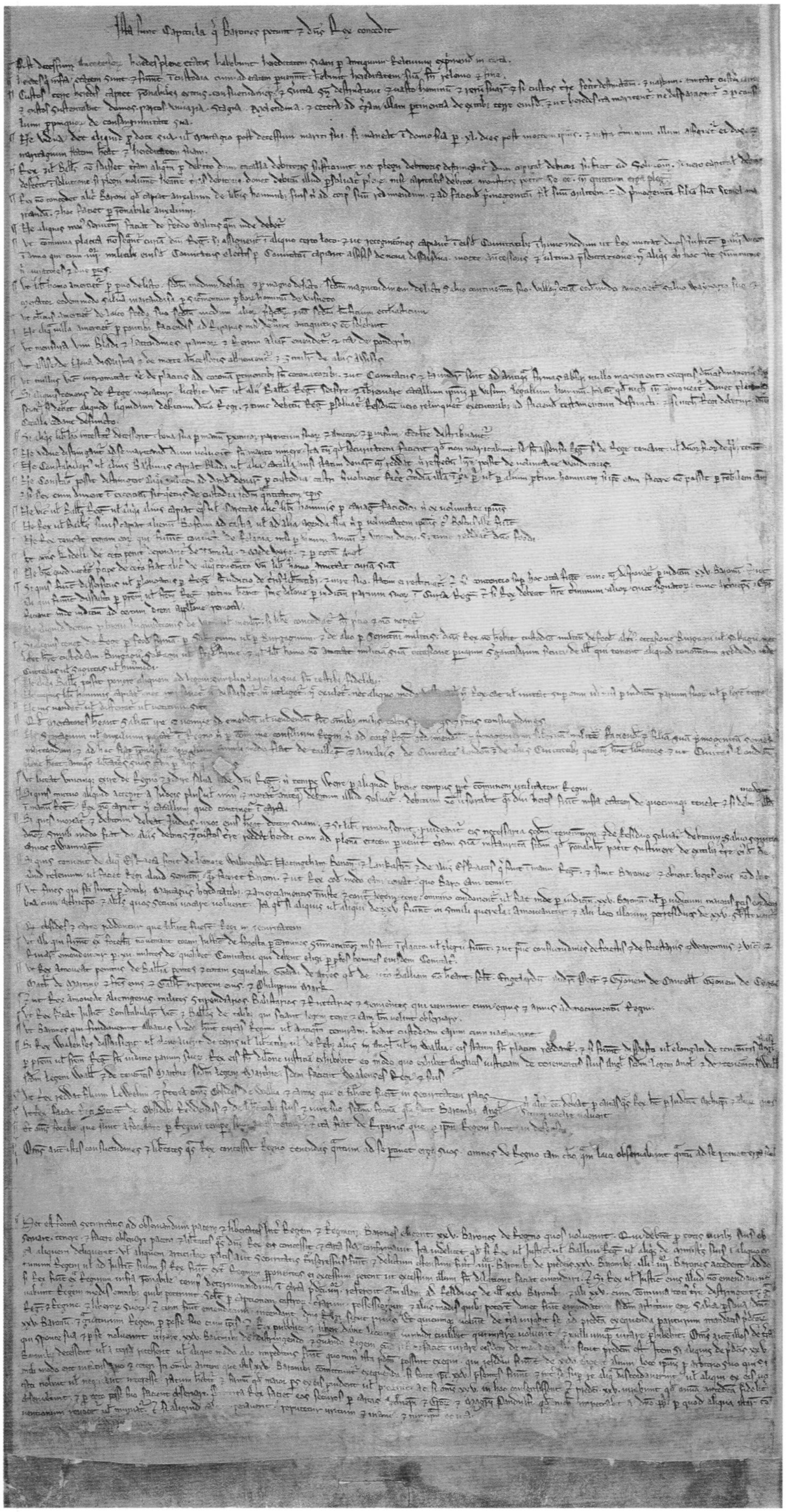

M agna Carta is – at first sight – a disappointing document. Unlike, say, the Declaration of Independence, it contains no sweeping statements of general principle. It was in origin a treaty between King John and his rebellious barons, and is concerned with fine points of feudal law.

However, Magna Carta established for the first time a constitutional principle of immense significance, namely that the power of the king could be limited by a written grant. As one historian has put it: 'Magna Carta is a landmark in the transition from an oral to a written society. It was not the first "charter of liberties" but by reason of its comprehensiveness and minuteness it became the practical starting point of our history.'

King John's unsuccessful attempts to defend his dominions in Normandy caused oppressive financial demands. Taxes were assessed in an extortionate fashion, with ruthless reprisals against defaulters. John's administration of justice was considered capricious. In January 1215, following a further disastrous campaign in France, a party of barons dressed in full armour appeared before John and demanded a charter of liberties as a safeguard against such arbitrary proceedings. John played for time; the barons took up arms against John, and captured London in May 1215. By 10 June, representatives of the King and the barons met at Runnymede, a field conveniently situated between the royal castle at Windsor and the baronial camp at Staines. Detailed negotiations ensued, and the document shown here, known as the Articles of the Barons, summarises the points which were agreed. The sealing of this document, presumably in John's presence, marked his formal acceptance of its terms.

British Library, Additional MS. 4838

Magna Carta

After the Articles of the Barons had been sealed, the royal chancery expanded and revised the text of the Articles, turning it into a formal royal grant. This grant afterwards became known as Magna Carta, the Great Charter, to distinguish it from the related Charter of the Forests, first issued in 1217. As a record of the grant, royal letters were issued containing a copy of its text. These letters were available shortly after the conclusion of the meeting at Runnymede on 21 June. Contemporary chronicles state that many of these letters were issued, but royal records refer to the dispatch of only thirteen. Four survive: two in the archives of the Deans and Chapters of Lincoln and Salisbury; and two at the British Library, one of which was badly damaged in a fire in 1731. These letters are the earliest record of the text of Magna Carta. This is the undamaged British Library letter, which, according to one account, was discovered in the 17th century in a London tailor's shop. The two most famous clauses of Magna Carta are as follows: 'No free man shall be seized or imprisoned, or stripped of his rights or possessions, or outlawed or exiled, or deprived of his standing in any other way, nor will we proceed with force against him, or send others to do so, except by the lawful judgement of his equals or by the law of the land.' 'To no one will we sell, to no one deny or delay right or justice.'

British Library, Cotton MS. Augustus ii.106

Even after the grant of Magna Carta, John's opponents did not trust him. They obliged him also to give them this document allowing the leaders of the nobility to continue to hold the city of London and the Tower as security until oaths had been administered to ensure that Magna Carta was observed. The barons' suspicion of John proved justified. At John's behest, the pope overturned Magna Carta as an unjust grant, plunging England into civil war. John died suddenly in 1216, with the issue unresolved. With the accession to the throne of John's nine-year-old son, Henry III, Magna Carta was revived as a manifesto by which moderate men might be converted to the young king's cause. It was reissued in 1216 and 1217, substantially revised to meet the altered circumstances of the new reign. In 1225, Magna Carta was reissued for a third time with smaller and, as events were to prove, final revisions, in return for the concession to the king of the right to levy a special tax. It was the 1225 revision which was to become the text of Magna Carta which later kings were repeatedly to confirm and which eventually found its way on to the statute books.

Public Record Office, C 47/34/1/1

Magna Carta

King John hunting, from a 14th-century collection of statutes produced in London.

British Library, Cotton MS. Claudius D .ii, f. 116

One of the most distinctive features of British, and particularly English, self-perception is the idea that national institutions have gradually evolved in an organic fashion over a long period. Although British history is marked by many major cataclysms, there is also a strong underlying administrative continuity. This is most powerfully expressed in the English public records, at the heart of which are record series which run in an unbroken sequence back to the beginning of the 13th century and which have remained in continuous official custody since that time. The 12th century saw an enormous increase in the use of written records to record land transfers and other administrative acts. The pipe rolls, recording royal accounts, had systematically been preserved since 1155, and in 1193–4 details of lawsuits heard by the royal court likewise began to be recorded. In 1195, Hubert Walter, Archbishop of Canterbury, introduced a new form of record which recorded court judgements in triplicate, so that both parties could have copies and a third be retained in the king's treasury. These experiments proved great successes, and encouraged the royal government to develop more systematic record-keeping. In the first year of King John's reign (1199–1200), the charter rolls were begun, which contained the official copies of solemn grants of land and other property. In the following year, the close rolls were introduced, which consisted of copies of

Shown here are three of the earliest government records: the first charter roll (1199-1200), the first *Curia Regis* (court of the king) roll (1193-1194), and the first patent roll (1201-1202). The rolls comprise pieces of parchment which were sewn together to form either a long continuous scroll or a kind of 'flip-chart'. The roll format was preferred over the book because the king's court frequently travelled long distances, and rolls could readily be placed in chests and transported by boat or wagon.

Public Record Office, KB 26/1; C 54/1; C 66/1

Recording Government

The growth of the use of written documents in everyday life during the 12th century is vividly reflected in this illustration from a life of St Guthlac, dating from about 1210, which shows benefactors of Crowland Abbey in Lincolnshire placing records of their gifts on the altar of the abbey. Behind the altar, a demon is shown leaving a sick man who has been cured by the power of St Guthlac.

British Library, Harley Roll Y.6

royal letters which had been sealed up to protect their confidentiality. The other major record of royal letters, the patent rolls, comprising copies of more public letters which had a seal at the foot of the document, was started in the third year of John's reign (1201–1202). Other important series, such as the fine rolls, recording details of payments due to the king, were also begun at this time. The patent rolls are still compiled, but are now just one of the thousands of record classes produced by the different branches of government.

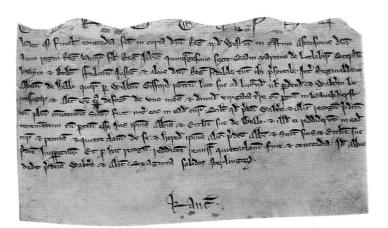

A tripartite final concord, to give it its technical name, comprised three copies of a judgement by the royal court on a lawsuit. These three parts of a final concord of 3 June 1272 record agreement made in a suit about land at Hawkhurst, Kent, between the Abbot of Battle and Walter le Messager. The wavy line created when cutting up the document into three parts was intended to provide a means of guarding against forgeries – the authenticity of one part could be established by matching the copies held by the parties against the official copy. From the 14th century final concords record fictitious suits and were used to legalise land conveyances.

Public Record Office, CP 25/1/98/55/1167; E 210/162 and 163

Westminster Abbey is the national church of Britain. Since 1066, royal coronations have taken place in the abbey, and until the time of George II, many English monarchs were buried there. However, Westminster Abbey is neither a great cathedral nor a particularly ancient foundation. Its prestige derives from ancient royal patronage and its proximity to the royal palace of Westminster. The history of Westminster Abbey therefore reflects the symbiotic relationship of church and state in Britain. The origins of the Abbey are obscure; it was refounded by St Dunstan in the 10th century and rebuilt in a lavish fashion by Edward the Confessor, who first established Westminster as a major seat of royal power. Edward apparently favoured this desolate marshy spot because it lay just outside the precincts of the troublesome city of London. His canonisation encouraged monarchs to associate themselves with him by being crowned at Westminster. Henry III (1207–72) was particularly devoted to St Edward, and at enormous expense rebuilt the abbey in the most up-to-date gothic style.

Henry III's close association with Westminster Abbey dates from 1220, when on 16 May the teenaged king laid the foundation stone of a new lady chapel there. The following day, Henry was crowned in the abbey, and gave the abbot a pair of gold spurs used in the coronation as a contribution towards the work on the new chapel. Henry's gift was recorded on the close roll (the first entry in this illustration). The monks found it difficult to finish the chapel from their own resources, and Henry gave them further help in the 1240s to complete the work. Henry's involvement in the building of the chapel seems to have inspired him to rebuild the whole abbey, a scheme inaugurated in 1245.
Public Record Office, C 54/24, m. 20

The medieval chronicler, Matthew Paris, a monk of St Albans, prefaced his *History of the English*, written in the 1250s, with a series of pictures of the post-Conquest kings, including this portait of Henry III, who is shown with a representation of Westminster Abbey in his hand.
British Library, Royal MS. 14.C.VII, f. 9

The Tower of London

The Tower of London was built by King William the Conqueror and his son, William Rufus, between 1077 and 1097 to help keep the city of London under control. The distinctive White Tower at the centre of the fortifications was part of this original Norman building. The Tower continued to be altered

During the 13th and 14th centuries, when there was a risk of an attack on London by the French, as well as occasional serious unrest, defensive enclosures were built around the Norman fortifications. This set of accounts records an extension of the south wall across the moat in Richard II's reign. The highly skilled masons working on the new wall earned 9s 3d a day. The carpenters used on some of the work earned just 10d a day.

Public Record Office, E 101/473/2, m.5

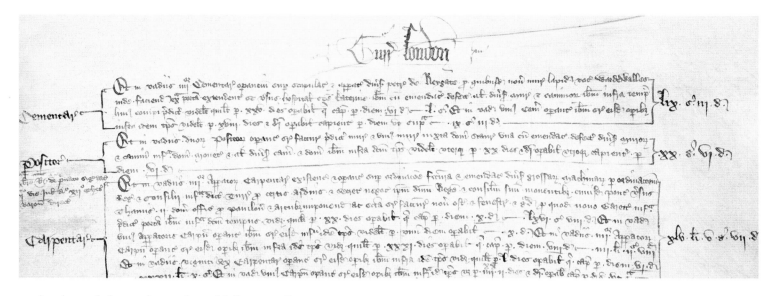

and enlarged throughout the middle ages. It had many different uses apart from the purely military. It served as a repository for records and other royal treasures. Until recently the Tower was the home of the Royal Armouries Museum, reputedly the largest collection of weaponry in the world. From Norman times until 1834, the Tower was also the home of the royal menagerie. It is best known, however, as a prison for high-profile captives. Amongst those held there were Sir Thomas More, Anne Boleyn, Lady Jane Grey and Sir Walter Raleigh. The last person so imprisoned was the senior Nazi Rudolf Hess.

Charles, Duke of Orléans (1391–1465) was commander of the French forces at the Battle of Agincourt (1415), where he was captured and taken to England. Among his various places of residence during his 25-year captivity was the Tower. While he was a prisoner, he wrote hundreds of beautiful short French poems. This Flemish manuscript of his poems, begun for Edward IV but uncompleted on his death in 1483 and not finished until the time of Henry VII, contains this miniature showing Charles in the White Tower, with Old London Bridge in the distance. It is the earliest surviving depiction of the Tower.

British Library, Royal MS. 16 F.II, f. 73

Simon de Montfort, 6th Earl of Leicester, was revered in the 19th century as the effective founder of parliament and a forefather of democracy, but he was also in many ways a self-seeking adventurer. His father had led the ferocious crusade against the Albigensians in southern France, and Simon celebrated his accession to the Earldom of Leicester by expelling the Jews from Leicester. A brother-in-law of Henry III, he became increasingly contemptuous of the pious and cultured Henry. In 1258, he was the leading force behind an attempt to invest power in a council of the nobility. By 1263, de Montfort was the leader of the noble movement against the king. In May 1264, at the Battle of Lewes he defeated and captured both Henry and his son Edward, and became effective ruler of England. He summoned knights and burgesses to a parliament in January 1265, but his overbearing behaviour alienated many. In August 1265, he was defeated and killed by Prince Edward at the Battle of Evesham.

The claim of Henry III to the French lands lost by his father John and his position as Duke of Aquitaine made for constant tension with the French king during the first part of his reign. In 1258, de Montfort and four other envoys negotiated a truce between Henry III and the French ruler Louis IX. This is a copy of the letters confirming the truce, to which impressions of the seals of the commissioners were attached sometime afterwards. De Montfort's seal is the large one on the right. The truce with France gave de Montfort and his allies a chance to pursue their plans to restrict Henry III's power, and within a few days of this peace being agreed, the 'Provisions of Oxford' were promulgated, whereby a baronial council was appointed to control the King more closely. Henry III said at the time that he feared de Montfort 'more than all the thunder and lightning in the world'.
British Library, Additional Charter 11297

The description of the Battle of Evesham in this 14th-century chronicle compiled at St Albans Abbey was accompanied by a vivid drawing of the battle, which was considered particularly savage, even by medieval standards. After he had been killed, de Montfort's body was dismembered, presumably to prevent a cult developing. Nevertheless, it was afterwards reported that miracles had been performed at his grave at Evesham Abbey and his followers made pilgrimages there.
British Library, Cotton MS. Nero D. ii, f. 177

The Mother of Parliaments

The word parliament, from the French *parlement* or 'discussion', was first used in the 13th century to describe meetings of nobles summoned by the king to discuss political, administrative and judicial questions. Assemblies of this kind were common all over medieval Europe. The English parliament is chiefly remarkable for its longevity. From the late 13th century, the practice began of summoning gentry and burgesses to these gatherings, and an unusual bi-cameral structure emerged, with a House of Lords containing hereditary lay peers and spiritual dignitaries and a House of Commons comprising representatives of shires and boroughs. The need for money to finance the wars against France in the 14th century gave parliament, and the Commons in particular, great political leverage, and parliamentary consent to taxation and new legislation became increasingly well-established principles.

The election of representatives of the gentry to parliament was ordered by a royal writ, which was returned endorsed with the names of the nominees who would attend the parliament. This is the oldest surviving such writ and return, issued in December 1274 for the election of members of parliament from Bedfordshire and Buckinghamshire to attend a parliament to be held at Easter 1275. Writs of this kind are still issued for the election of MPs today.
Public Record Office, C 219/1/1/1

The enhanced prestige and power of parliament by the end of the 14th century is apparent from the central role it played in the political crises of Richard II's reign. When Richard was finally captured by Henry Bolingbroke and coerced into abdicating, the lords of parliament assembled on 30 September 1399 at Westminster Hall around an empty throne and accepted his resignation. Henry then seated himself in the throne. This miniature from a manuscript of an account of the fall of Richard by Jean Creton, a member of his retinue, shows the scene at Westminster, with the lords gathered around the empty throne.
British Library, Harley MS. 1319, f. 57

This illustration of St Andrew is taken from the Gorleston Psalter, a lavishly illustrated manuscript produced in East Anglia in the early 14th century for the parish church of the village of Gorleston, near Great Yarmouth in Norfolk.

British Library, Additional MS. 49622, f. 11v

St George, the patron saint of England, was martyred at Lydda in Palestine in about 330. He was probably a soldier, but this is not certain. The famous story of George rescuing a princess by slaying a dragon which was going to eat her, a feat which he performed in return for the conversion of the princess's people, was made popular by the 13th-century compilation of saints' lives, *The Golden Legend*. George came to be regarded as a special patron of soldiers during the crusades, and Richard I and his army placed themselves under his protection. St George was seen as the perfect embodiment of the ideals of christian chivalry, and when in 1348 Edward III founded the order of the garter, the most ancient chivalric order in Europe, he placed it under the patronage of St George. This picture of a garter king of arms kneeling before the saint is from an armorial containing portraits of the founder-knights of the order of the garter, made for William Bruges, the first garter king of arms, in about 1430. In 1415, following the Battle of Agincourt, the feast of St George (23 April) was established as one of the principal festivals of the English Church. With the invention of gunpowder and the decline of the knightly ideal, devotion to St George declined on the continent, but he remained popular in England.

British Library, Stowe MS. 594, f. 5v

St Patrick, the patron saint of Ireland, was born in about 390 somewhere on the west coast of Britain. As a youth he was captured by Irish pirates and became a slave. As he tended his master's herds, he prayed and dreamed of freedom. After six years, he either escaped or was set free, and made his way to the coast, where he persuaded some sailors to take him home. After many adventures, he finally rejoined his family, and decided to train as a priest. He was sent to Ireland as a bishop in about 435, set up a see at Armagh, and established a firm organisational structure for the Irish Church. From Armagh, he engaged in missionary work and encouraged the growth of monasticism in Ireland. His writings show him as an attractive personality, humble, sincere, conscious of his own shortcomings, but with a complete trust in God. This 13th-century illustration of Patrick shows him asleep on a rock, watched over by Christ, while beneath the rock are sleeping animals, which represent the unconverted.

British Library, Royal MS. 20.D.VII, f. 213v

St David or Dewi Sant, the patron saint of Wales, is a 6th-century figure of whom little is known. His life was written by Rhygyfarch in the late 11th century, but this must be used with the utmost caution. For example, Rhygyfarch's claim that David was a grandson of Ceredig, king of Ceredigion, must almost certainly be rejected. On the other hand, David's original sphere of activity was clearly south Cardiganshire and north Pembrokeshire, with *Vallis Rosina*, the present-day St David's, early achieving primacy among the sites connected with him. His sobriquet *Dyfrwr*, 'water-drinker', is also early and may indicate that his monks followed a notably ascetic way of life. He is thought to have died on 1 March 589.

His cult spread from south-west Wales to the English border and the west of England. There are also churches dedicated to him in Cornwall and Brittany, and his fame soon spread to Ireland as well. He was proclaimed a saint by Pope Callistus II (1119–24) and from 1398 onwards (and especially from 1415 onwards) his feast day of 1 March was celebrated with due solemnity in the province of Canterbury. This custom lapsed after the Reformation, but was revived in the 18th century, and St David's Day is now widely celebrated worldwide by Welsh people and those of Welsh descent. Shown here is part of the Office of St David of Menevia from the mid-14th century Penpont Antiphonal. It is a rhymed office together with chants in honour of St David, and is the only proper office known to celebrate the memory of a Welsh saint.

National Library of Wales, NLW MS 20541E, f. 205r

Llywelyn ap Grufydd (c. 1228–1282) was a grandson of Llywelyn ap Iorwerth, 'the Great', and, partly thanks to the political turmoil in England at the end of of Henry III's reign, created a principality that was larger than his grandfather's. Llywelyn's territorial gains were reluctantly accepted by the English in the Treaty of Montgomery in 1267, which also confirmed him as Prince of Wales, the first and last time that the English recognised a native holder of this title. Edward I, as Llywelyn's overlord, was determined to bring Llywelyn to heel and Llywelyn was condemned as a rebel for failure to do homage to Edward and other alleged misdemeanours. In 1276–7, Edward overwhelmed Llywelyn and forced him to accept a humiliating peace. Edward started to create a network of extremely large and imposing castles to ensure the complete subjugation of the Welsh. The oppressive behaviour of the English quickly created great resentment, and in 1282 a war of national liberation started. Edward's men conquered Gwynedd and Llywelyn was killed. In 1284, by the Statute of Rhuddlan, Edward imposed a colonial settlement on Wales. English legal procedures were extensively introduced and towns established which were inhabited by English settlers. Edward's heir was born at Caernarfon Castle and was made Prince of Wales, a title thereafter always used by the monarch's eldest son.

This exchequer roll itemising payments by the wardrobe, the office of the royal household which financed Edward's military expenditure, gives details of the installation of a great military ballista at Caenarfon Castle in December 1282. Edward intended that Caernarfon should be the administrative centre of north Wales.

Public Record Office, E 101/351/9, m. 9

A watercolour by Julius Caesar Ibbetson (1759–1817) of Conwy Castle, dated 1796, portraying John Smith, the blind harpist at the height of his career. The Reverend Richard Warner, visiting the town in 1797, mentions Conwy as the best place to hear fine harp music. The castle, begun in 1283, to secure and safeguard the Conwy Valley for Edward I, survives today as one of the most impressive medieval buildings in Wales.

National Library of Wales

Scotland : The Wars of Independence

On a stormy night in March 1286 King Alexander III of Scotland was thrown by his horse over a cliff at Kinghorn in Fife, leaving as his only direct heir his three year old granddaughter who lived in Norway. Her death four years later on the journey to Scotland sparked off a succession crisis. The six guardians appointed to govern Scotland after Alexander's death invited Edward I of England to resolve the claims of the thirteen competitors for the crown. In 1292 he made his judgement in favour of the hapless John Balliol who gave homage to the English king.

Edward used any opportunity to assert his position as overlord of Scotland and Balliol's feudal superior. When he demanded the service of the Scots for his wars against the French, however, relations between the two countries broke down entirely. In 1295, having removed Balliol for failing to stand up to Edward, the Scots negotiated an alliance with the French in a treaty which formed the basis of the Auld Alliance. Edward invaded the following March, crushed Scottish resistance, imprisoned Balliol and set up his own administration to govern the country. The symbols of Scottish nationhood – the regalia, records and the Stone of Destiny

The Treaty of Birgham/Northampton, 18 July 1290, set out the terms of the marriage arranged between Alexander III's grand-daughter, known as the 'Maid of Norway', and Edward I's son. Many safeguards were written into the treaty to protect Scotland's independence. Two months after the sealing of the treaty, the bride-to-be died on her way to Scotland.
National Archives of Scotland, SP 6/1

During the 16 months it took to reach a decision over the succession to the Scottish throne, Edward acted as lord paramount of Scotland, issuing documents under the seal of the Guardians of Scotland. The seal shows St Andrew on the saltire cross and bears the inscription, 'Saint Andrew be leader of the compatriot Scots'.
National Archives of Scotland, RH 5/55

English claims to the overlordship of Scotland continued even after their comprehensive defeat at Bannockburn. This letter from the earls and barons of Scotland to Pope John XXII, better known as the Declaration of Arbroath, forcibly and eloquently puts forward the case for Scottish independence: 'It is in truth not for glory, nor riches, nor honours that we are fighting, but for freedom – for that alone, which no honest man gives up but with life itself.' It asks the pope to persuade Edward II to leave the Scots in peace. The pope finally recognised Bruce as king of an independent Scotland in 1324.

National Archives of Scotland, SP 13/7

upon which the Scottish monarchs were crowned – were taken to England as trophies of war. The Ragman Rolls, named after the term for a long piece of parchment, record the submission of hundreds of Scots who did homage to Edward.

Stung by the humiliation of the English occupation, armed resistance broke out led by William Wallace and Sir Andrew Moray. Their army inflicted a crushing defeat on the English at Stirling Bridge in 1297, only to be defeated the following year at Falkirk. A period of diplomatic activity ensued as the Scots tried to persuade the French and the papacy to put

pressure on Edward, but by 1304 he had reasserted his supremacy over Scotland. After Wallace's capture and execution in 1305, Robert the Bruce emerged as the only leader capable of uniting the Scots in their struggle for independence. Crowned King of Scots in 1306, he began a long drawn out campaign of guerilla warfare culminating in 1314 in a major tactical victory at Bannockburn.

Bannockburn did not bring the war to an end however. Edward II did not renounce his claim to Scottish overlordship and refused to recognise Bruce as legitimate king. The Declaration of Arbroath, a letter written to the

Scotland : The Wars of Independence

Contemporary portrait of Edward I, apparently hearing a lawsuit. At the foot of the throne, three clerks record details of the proceedings.
British Library, Cotton MS. Vitellius A. xiii, f. 6v

papacy in 1320 setting out the case for independence, initiated a round of diplomatic attempts to establish peace between the two countries which finally came with the Treaty of Edinburgh in March 1328. The first War of Independence had ended, but the 'perpetual peace' established by the treaty broke down four years later. The hostility between the 'old enemies' only came to an end with another Treaty of Edinburgh in 1560.

'Alasse, Dethe, Alasse'

The Black Death was a watershed in medieval history. This pandemic of bubonic plague, spread both by fleas on rats and from person to person by sneezing, began in central Asia and reached Italy from Constantinople in October 1347. A Gascon sailor who landed at the port of Melcombe Regis in June 1348 brought the disease to England. By the end of 1349, it had spread through the entire British Isles, with the exception of some remote parts of Ireland. There are no precise figures of the number of people who died. The best guess is that the population of England, which was about 5 or 6 million in 1347, was reduced to 3 million. Moreover, further smaller outbreaks of plague continued to occur for many years after 1349, so that the population continued to decline throughout the rest of the 14th century. The social and economic consequences of this catastrophic loss of population were immense. Although few communities were completely wiped out, property values fell and it was difficult for lords to insist on tenants performing their customary services, so that the tenurial system began to unravel. Labourers were able to demand higher wages and move about more freely. Many towns suffered a loss of trade and population. The psychological impact of this terrible event was enormous, and is reflected in an increased popular preoccupation with mortality during the late 14th and 15th centuries.

On 1 August 1349, the aged Bishop of Worcester died and for three months, until a new bishop was consecrated, the estates of the bishopric were in the hands of the crown. The text shown is the beginning of the record on an exchequer memoranda roll of the audit of the accounts of the officials who administered the bishop's estates while they were in royal custody. These show the devastating effects of the Black Death on some villages. At Hanbury (the village which has achieved more recent fame as the model for Ambridge in the radio series *The Archers*), the number of tenants fell from more than 60 to just four.
Public Record Office, E 368/124, m. 259

Images of death pervade the art of post-plague England. Not only are images of mortality more frequent than before the plague, but they are more explicit in their depiction of death and decay. These portrayals of death are taken from an illustrated collection of English religious texts compiled by a Carthusian monk in Yorkshire in the 15th century.
British Library, Additional MS. 37049, ff. 31v, 38v

'Who was then the gentleman?'

The Peasants' Revolt of 1381 was the most extensive and successful popular rebellion in medieval England. The revolt was provoked by heavy-handed attempts to enforce the payment of a poll tax, a flat-rate payment by every person which was more onerous for the poor than the rich. The government failed to bring initial disturbances in Kent and Essex under control, and insurgents from those counties made a concerted movement towards London, with Wat Tyler emerging as leader of the Kentish rebels. The insurgents entered London, where they sacked John of Gaunt's palace of the Savoy, stormed the Tower of London, and captured and executed Simon Sudbury, the Archbishop of Canterbury and Chancellor of England, Robert Hales, the Treasurer of England and Prior of the Hospitallers, and other royal officials. The rising spread as far afield as York and Somerset, with particularly serious disturbances throughout the Home Counties and East Anglia. Wat Tyler was killed by the Mayor of London, William Walworth, during a meeting with King Richard II at Smithfield, and the revolt collapsed soon afterwards.

The rebels released from prison the veteran radical preacher John Ball, who preached to the insurgents as they assembled at Blackheath before entering London. He took as his text the couplet: 'When Adam delved and Eve span\Who was then the gentleman?' This depiction of Ball preaching to the rebels is taken from a 15th-century Flemish manuscript of John Froissart's *Chronicles*.
British Library, Royal MS. 18. E.I, f. 165v.

After the death of Tyler, commissions were set up for the whole country to arrest and punish the rebels. This indictment was taken by the Earl of Suffolk's commission against the rebels in Norfolk and Suffolk. Among the incidents it describes are attacks on the Earl's own properties at Bawdsey and Hollesley in Suffolk, in which all the charters, rolls and other documents which recorded details of the services owed by the Earl's tenants were burnt. Above the name of one of the rebels, John Reynold, is a note 'Decollat', indicating that he was beheaded as a traitor by the commission.
Public Record Office, KB 9/166/1, m. 24

The language of government, church and literature in medieval Europe was Latin. Pre-conquest England was unusual, however, in that Old English, a Germanic language at first sight largely incomprehensible to modern English speakers, was extensively used both for literature and for a wide variety of administrative purposes. With the Norman Conquest and the arrival of a French-speaking nobility, Latin and French became established as the normal means of official communication.

During the 12th and 13th centuries, English underwent a radical transformation. Many Old English words were replaced by words derived from French and many new French loan words were introduced. Methods of spelling and pronouncing the language also fundamentally changed. The resulting language is known by philologists as Middle English. Middle English began to be used increasingly by writers, and great poets such as Geoffrey Chaucer and William Langland, writing at the end of the 14th century, showed that literature in English could be as fine as that in French or Latin.

Another factor in the rise of English was its use in local cultural events, such as the civic cycles of mystery plays performed in the streets of various towns on the feast of Corpus Christi (the Thursday after Trinity Sunday). The mystery plays consisted of a series of individual pageants performed by a particular group of craftsmen or 'mystery'. The plays enacted the events of the Bible from the Creation to the Ascension (or, in some cases, the Day of Judgement). The most famous cycle of mystery plays was that performed at York, which comprised over fifty pageants, all performed in one day. Each pageant was performed on an elaborately decorated wagon at different stations in the streets of the city. The earliest reference to the performance of York plays is in 1376. After the Reformation, these performances began to be seen as idolatrous, and the plays were discontinued. This manuscript, written between 1463 and 1477, is the official record of the text of the York plays compiled for the town council. Shown here is part of the glovers' play of Cain and Abel.

British Library, Additional MS.35290, f. 23v

The Bannatyne Manuscript, named after the Edinburgh merchant George Bannatyne (b. 1545) who compiled it around 1568, is the largest and most important Scottish poetic anthology of its period. A few of the poems are English, but the great majority are by Scots and in Scots, the language of the southern and eastern part of the kingdom of Scotland. Although deriving like Middle English from Old English, and most closely related to the northern dialect of that, it was by the 14th century a linguistically as well as politically separate language, and had replaced Gaelic and Norman French as tongue of government and court. The earliest poem in Scots is John Barbour's *Brus* (1376), but the major period for poetry was the century from 1450 to 1550. The names of Robert Henryson, William Dunbar, Gavin Douglas and Sir David Lindsay are the best known among a great host of writers in all poetic genres. The section of the Bannatyne Manuscript shown here contains the beginning of Sir David Lindsay's *Ane Satyre of the thrie estaitis*, staged at Cupar in 1552.

National Library of Scotland, Adv. MS. 1.1.6, f. 168

Geoffrey Chaucer: The Poet as Civil Servant

Geoffrey Chaucer (c. 1343–1400) played a fundamental role in developing English as a literary language, and the personalities and imagery of his greatest work, *The Canterbury Tales*, played a vital part in shaping English self-perceptions. Chaucer earned his living as a civil servant, so the public records provide many details about his life. A page to the Countess of Ulster, daughter-in-law of Edward III in 1357, he was a member of the English army in France in 1359, and was taken prisoner and ransomed. By 1366, he had joined the royal household as an esquire, and married Philippa, one of the queen's ladies-in-waiting. Having taken part in diplomatic missions to France and Italy (where he discovered the works of Dante and Boccaccio), he went on to become a senior customs official (1374–86), clerk of the king's works (1389–91), a justice of the peace and member of parliament for Kent – but also survived near-bankruptcy in 1388. Although Chaucer is best known for *The Canterbury Tales*, a series of stories told in the course of a pilgrimage from Southwark to Canterbury, he also composed a number of other major works, including *Troilus and Creseyde*, *The House of Fame* and *The Book of the Duchess*. Many of his poems were probably first recited at the royal court, but they also circulated widely in manuscript, showing that they gained immediate popularity. Chaucer's prestige has remained undimmed to the present day; his friend Thomas Hoccleve described him as 'the first finder of our fair language', while later writers acclaimed him as the English Homer.

A number of petitions and account rolls relating to Chaucer's work as a customs officer survive, such as this 1385 petition requesting permission for Chaucer to appoint a deputy to help him in his work. These documents are in different hands. It is probable that one of these hands is Chaucer's, but it is impossible to say which.
Public Record Office, C 81/1394/87

When Chaucer died, *The Canterbury Tales* were incomplete, and the final order of the tales not settled. Although 88 manuscripts of the poem survive, the differences between them are often considerable, and scholars have laboured to try and establish a text as close to Chaucer's intentions as possible. Many scholars regard the text of this manuscript, known as the Hengwrt Chaucer, as one of the earliest and most reliable of the poem. Shown here is the opening of the Summoner's Tale. This manuscript belongs to the Peniarth collection (formerly called Hengwrt), the most important of the foundation collections of the National Library of Wales. The origins of the Peniarth collection lie in the strenuous efforts of the 17th-century antiquary Robert Vaughan of Hengwrt, a country house near Dolgellau, to rescue manuscripts threatened at that time with destruction.
National Library of Wales, Peniarth MS. 392, f. 79v.

Chaucer is the first English writer for whom we possess reasonably life-like portraits. This seems to be the result of the initiative of Chaucer's friend, the poet Thomas Hoccleve, who arranged for pictures of Chaucer to be drawn so that his appearance should be remembered. This portrait of Chaucer is taken from an early manuscript of *The Canterbury Tales*.
British Library, Lansdowne MS. 851, f. 2

In the 1340s, Edward III made a formal claim to the French throne and inflicted a series of humiliating defeats on the French. From 1369 onwards, however, the French generally had the upper hand in this struggle, which came to be known as the Hundred Years War, and in 1396 Richard II agreed to a long-term truce. Henry V, perhaps anxious to demonstrate his right to occupy the English throne seized by his father from Richard, renewed the attacks on the French. In 1415, Henry captured the port of Harfleur, then marched across Normandy towards Calais. He met a much larger French force near the village nowadays known as Azincourt. The overconfident French launched a full-scale assault on Henry, and were cut to pieces by his archers. This victory enabled Henry to conquer Normandy. William Shakespeare vividly portrayed Agincourt as an archetypal victory of 'the few', fighting with their backs to the wall in a just cause against overwhelming odds, and thus assured Agincourt a central place in the English national myth.

Henry V and his father were skilful at using many different types of propaganda to exalt their rule and emphasise their identity with the interests of the nation. Many songs and popular ballads appeared which gave disproportionately inflated accounts of the glories of Agincourt. This song praises the virtues of St George, and describes how he helped put the French to flight. It comes from a manuscript compiled probably at St George's chapel, Windsor, between 1430 and 1444.
British Library, Egerton MS. 3307, f. 63v

This roll contains the detailed expense claims of those who followed Henry V to France in 1415. Shown here is part of the account of William Kynwolmerssh, the cofferer of the king's household. The archers who joined William on the campaign were paid six pence a day, the men at arms twelve pence a day.
Public Record Office, E 358/6 m. 3

William Caxton

William Caxton (d. 1491) was a successful mercer based in London. In 1462, he was appointed to the prestigious post of governor of the commercial association known as the Merchant Adventurers at Bruges, which gave him an important role in regulating English trade with the Low Countries. As a leisure activity, he translated a popular romance from French to English, and, finding that his friends and acquaintances were fascinated by the book, decided to produce numerous copies by the newly discovered method of printing, which he had seen in Bruges. He visited Cologne to find out how printing worked, and in 1473 set up a printing shop in Bruges. The first book he produced at Bruges, and the first book to be printed in English, was his translation, entitled *Recuyell of the Historyes of Troye*. In 1476, he moved to Westminster and thereafter devoted himself to printing and translating, producing more than a hundred titles.

Among the first items printed by Caxton after his return from Bruges to England in 1476 was this form, whereby the Abbot of Abingdon in the Pope's name promises that the recipients will avoid all punishment for their sins, because they had given money to support a fleet against the Turks. This particular copy was issued on 13 December 1476 to Henry and Katherine Lanley of London, and is the earliest known piece of printing from England.
Public Record Office, E 135/6/56

Caxton's output as both translator and printer was remarkable, and much of Caxton's work played a fundamental role in shaping national perceptions. For example, his printing of Malory's *Morte d'Arthur* popularised Malory's brilliant recasting of the Arthur legend, and helped ensure that the name of Arthur lived beyond the middle ages. This is the only surviving manuscript of Malory's work. Traces of ink on the manuscript show that it was in fact the one used by Caxton in printing this work.
British Library, Additional MS. 59678, f. 45

Caxton's monogram and initials. The appearance is reminiscent of the marks used by medieval merchants to label their goods.

Richard III was one of the unluckiest kings in English history, in that he suffered posthumous character assassination by two masters of the English language, Thomas More and William Shakespeare. Recent research suggests that Richard was not the shifty, acquisitive schemer that Shakespeare portrayed. Following the death of Edward IV, who had seized the throne from the weak Henry VI, Richard took the heir to the throne, Edward V, into his custody, supposedly to protect him. However, Edward and his brother, who became known as the 'Princes in the Tower', disappeared. Whether they were murdered by Richard or not has never been established. But contemporary suspicions that they had been prompted a rising against the king, leading eventually to his defeat and death in 1485. This drawing of Richard III is taken from a profusely illustrated chronicle in roll form compiled by a Warwickshire chantry priest, John Rous, and commemorating the patrons of his chapel, the holders of the earldom of Warwick. Richard, crowned in full armour and surrounded by heraldic crests, is shown together with his wife, Queen Anne (Neville), and his son Edward.

British Library, Additional MS. 48976

When Richard III was defeated by Henry Tudor at the Battle of Bosworth in 1485, the struggle between various descendants of Edward III for the English throne came to an end. It was said that the white rose, associated with Edmund Langley, Duke of York and Edward IV, had been avenged by the red rose, the emblem of the Lancastrians who traced their claim to the throne through John of Gaunt and Henry IV. This was a reference to the supposed death of the Yorkist 'Princes in the Tower' at the hands of Richard III. This imagery led to the development of the term 'Wars of the Roses', which came to be applied to all the various wars for possession of the English crown from 1450. Under Henry VII, the Tudor rose became a potent national symbol, as is reflected in this musical canon in honour of Henry VIII and celebrating the union of the Houses of York and Lancaster.

British Library, Royal MS. 11 F.XI, f. 2v

Tudors and Stuarts

The fifteenth passes with drums and in armour:
the monk watches it through the mind's grating.

The sixteenth puts on its cap and bells
to poach vocabulary from a king's laughter.

The seventeenth wears a collar of lace
at its neck, the flesh running from thought's candle.

R. S. Thomas, *Centuries*

The medieval Church was international; as a result of the religious reforms of the 16th century, the Churches of Britain became national, and in each of the British nations the reformed Church played a fundamental role in developing and preserving a sense of national community. In England, Henry VIII, frustrated in his attempts to secure a divorce, listened willingly to those who argued that he should be the supreme head of an English Church. The Pope's authority was abolished by act of parliament, the monasteries were suppressed and their land seized, and an English translation of the Bible was authorised. Shortly after Henry's death, the Church began holding its services in English. Queen Mary briefly tried to reintroduce Catholicism, but under Elizabeth the Church of England was firmly established as a Protestant church using an English Bible and prayer book, whose language played an important part in fostering the remarkable literary activity of Elizabethan England, including most famously the plays of William Shakespeare, which have come to be regarded as among the greatest treasures of the English cultural inheritance.

Ship from Henry VIII's navy.
British Library, Additional MS. 22047

Between 1536 and 1543, England finally completed the annexation of Wales by means of statutes passed by an English parliament containing no Welsh representatives. English-style shires were imposed on Wales, and Welsh outlawed as a legal language. However, as ecclesiastical reform proceeded, it became evident that it was necessary to have Bibles and prayer books in Welsh, and in 1563 parliament ordained that a Welsh translation of the Bible and the Book of Common Prayer should be produced. These translations became the foundation of modern Welsh literature and played a critical part in ensuring the survival of the Welsh language. In Scotland, the establishment of Protestantism resulted from a series of acts of defiance against the Crown, culminating in the abolition of papal jurisdiction, the banning of the mass and the passing of the Confession of Faith by the Scottish parliament in 1560. Joint actions such as these helped play an important part in fostering a sense of national solidarity.

Elizabeth I made no provision for her succession, so that when she died the unification of England and Scotland under a single ruler, James VI of Scotland and I of England, was almost accidental. Nevertheless, for the first time, the British mainland was ruled by a single person. However much James longed for a 'union of hearts and minds', England and Scotland remained uninterested in further unification. Instead, the absolutist views of royal authority which James espoused helped sow the seeds of war between the British kingdoms during the reign of his son Charles. Charles tried to impose a 'high church' prayer book on the Scottish Church, but the Scottish nobility and clergy rejected both the prayer book and the rule of bishops. The example of the Scots encouraged the English parliament to resist Charles over financial and religious issues. Charles tried to rule without the English Parliament, but was forced to recall it. The English Parliament entered into an alliance with the Scots against Charles. War broke out and the King was eventually captured and exiled. With the rise of Oliver Cromwell, the Scots supported Charles's son, Charles II, but were ruthlessly repressed by Cromwell.

The restoration of the monarchy under Charles II did not resolve these tensions. Charles declared himself a Catholic on his death bed; Charles's successor, his brother James II, had been openly Catholic for many years. James was overthrown in favour of William of Orange, but William's dismissive treatment of Scotland encouraged support for the Stuarts in Scotland and pointed the way to further conflict in the 18th century.

Until 1534, while constraints on the king of England's powers as head of state were few, in matters spiritual he was subject to the head of the Catholic Church, the pope in Rome. The English clergy and people paid taxes to the papacy and its representatives and the powers of parliament and the judges were limited by the laws of the Church. Hostility to this state of affairs had built up within England during the later middle ages, fuelled by the corruption of some late medieval popes. But it was the 'King's Great Matter' – his divorce from Catherine of Aragon, deemed necessary to allow him to marry Anne Boleyn and produce a

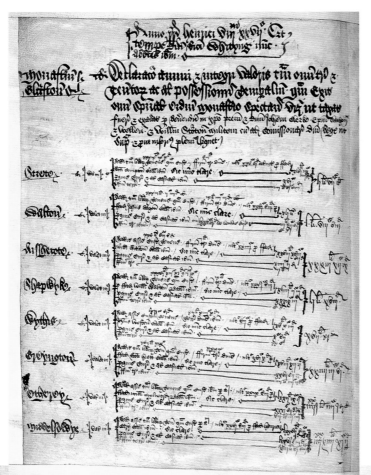

(left) The break with Rome had profound consequences on the English state and people. Those executed for their opposition to it included John Fisher, bishop of Rochester, three monks from the London Charterhouse, and most notably, Sir Thomas More, Henry's former Lord Chancellor. The new Church of England too underwent a seismic change when more than 800 monasteries were dissolved and their lands and wealth diverted into the royal coffers. The process began in 1535 when Thomas Cromwell, the King's principal advisor, carried out two surveys: the *Compendium Compertorum*, an inquiry into the spiritual health of the monasteries, and the *Valor Ecclesiasticus*, a survey of their lands and possessions. In 1536 the smaller houses in England and Wales were all closed down; the larger ones, under acute pressure from Cromwell and his minions, surrendered to the Crown more gradually until by early 1540 all had gone. Among the last was Glastonbury, whose abbot, the aged Richard Whiting, was dragged on a hurdle to the top of Glastonbury Tor and executed in November 1539. Glastonbury's wealth was assessed in the *Valor Ecclesiasticus* at more than £3,300, making it worth more than all the other Somerset monasteries combined, and one of the richest monasteries in England.

Public Record Office, E 344/14, f. 22v

The keystone of a series of measures passed by the Reformation Parliament, the Act of Supremacy sanctioned the transfer of authority from pope to king. With the other acts passed between November 1529 and April 1536, it enabled parliament the freedom to legislate on any subject. The bill is inscribed at the lower right hand corner to show that it was sent from the Lords to the Commons, who subsequently assented to it.

House of Lords Record Office, Original Act, 26 Henry VIII, no 1

Henry VIII and the Reformation

male heir – which brought about the split from Rome. Pope Clement VII, under pressure from Catherine's powerful kinsman the Emperor Charles V, refused to annul the marriage to Catherine, but the king's scholars furnished him with powerful arguments that the pope's jurisdiction was false and that he was the head of the Church of England by divine right. Convinced by these, it was to parliament that Henry turned, first in 1533 to cut off Rome's rights over justice and taxation, and then, in November 1534, to assert that he was the supreme head on earth of the English Church.

The religious houses were all obliged to acknowledge the royal supremacy: Glastonbury did so on 19 September 1534.
Public Record Office, E 25/57

Although some of the great monasteries, such as Gloucester Abbey, were refounded as cathedrals and their fabric thus preserved, in most cases the lands with their buildings were sold on by the Crown to local wealthy families who stripped the fabric bare and constructed new great houses. What Shakespeare described as the 'bare ruined choirs', left behind, have inspired profound melancholy and nostalgia down the generations, as here in this 19th-century view of the exterior of the ruined Lady Chapel at Glastonbury.
British Library, Additional MS. 17463, f. 135

Henry VIII and his Six Wives

Henry VIII (1491–1547) is celebrated in popular memory chiefly for his marital history, and even major events of his reign such as the Reformation of the English Church have been portrayed largely in terms of Henry's problems with his wives. After Henry's brother Arthur died, he married Arthur's widow, Catherine of Aragon, who proved herself an able queen, successfully acting as regent in Henry's absence. But Henry was unhappy that their only surviving child was a girl, Mary, and that he had no male heir. He fell in love with Anne Boleyn, and his attempts to secure a divorce from Catherine helped undermine relations with the papacy. Henry secretly married Anne in 1533, but again the marriage produced only a girl, Elizabeth. It was rumoured that Anne had committed adultery, and Henry fell in love with Jane Seymour. Anne was executed, and Henry married Jane, who at last gave birth to the long-awaited son, but died in childbirth. Henry was persuaded to marry Anne of Cleves for diplomatic reasons, but found her repulsive, and the marriage was annulled. Other court factions encouraged an alliance with Catherine Howard, but on this occasion it was Catherine who found Henry repulsive, and she sought sexual adventures elsewhere. Having executed her in 1542, Henry finally found contentment in his marriage in 1543 to the sympathetic and warm-hearted Catherine Parr, who outlived him.

Portrait of Henry VIII and his fool, Will Somers, from a psalter which was owned by Henry.
British Library, Royal MS. 2 A.XVI, f. 63v

This is the opening part of the record of the trial of Anne Boleyn before a group of peers of the realm in the Tower of London on trumped-up charges of treasonous adultery. Two juries in Kent and Middlesex were persuaded to approve indictments alleging that Anne had been engaged in sexual misconduct throughout her marriage, including (supposedly) incest with her brother Lord Rochford. Anne's alleged lovers had already been convicted of treason, so the result was a foregone conclusion. When Anne was executed on Tower Green, she was beheaded with a sword, a method of execution not used in England at that time, so the executioner of Calais was brought especially from France to carry out the sentence.
Public Record Office KB 8/9

Henry VIII and his Six Wives

Signatures of the six wives of Henry VIII:

Catherine of Aragon
(1485–1536)
*Public Record Office,
SP 1/5, no. 219*

Anne Boleyn (d. 1536)
*Public Record Office,
SP 1/53, no. 5422, i*

Jane Seymour (d. 1537)
*British Library, Cotton MS.
Vespasian F. iii, f. 36*

Anne of Cleves
(1515–57)
*Public Record Office,
SP 11/4, no. 18*

Catherine Howard
(1521–42)
*Public Record Office,
SP 1/167, p. 14*

Catherine Parr
(1512–48)
*Public Record Office,
SP 1/190, no. 221*

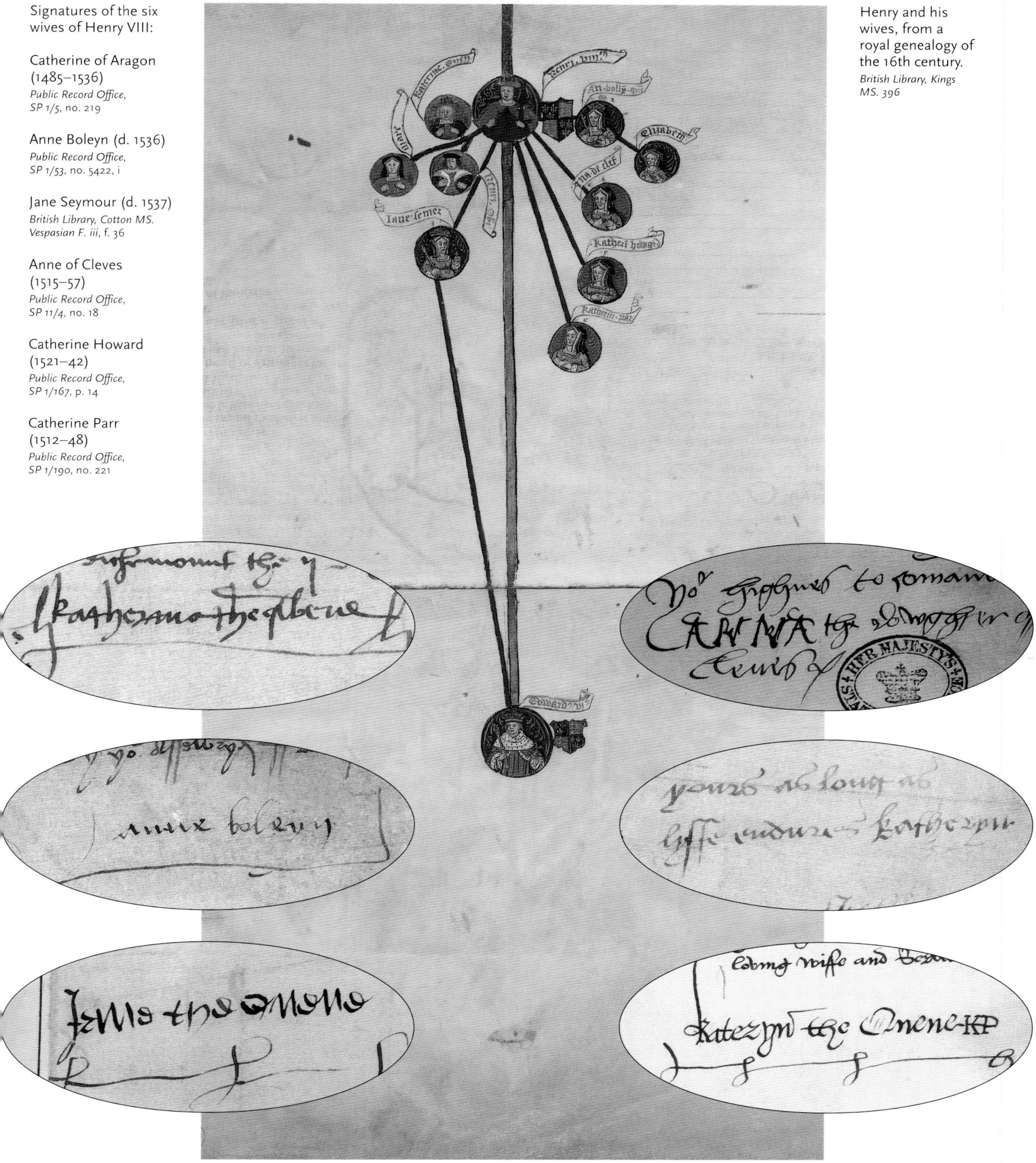

Henry and his wives, from a royal genealogy of the 16th century.
British Library, Kings MS. 396

The Church and the People

In the later Middle Ages, a major focus of popular dissatisfaction with the Church was its insistence that the language of the Bible and worship had to be Latin, accessible only to the educated elite. The Reformation saw an upsurge in vernacular translations of the Bible across Europe: Martin Luther published his seminal edition in German in 1522. William Tyndale, in exile in Germany and later the Low Countries, followed with an English New Testament in 1526, revised in 1534. Tyndale's New Testament was published by Peter Schoeffer in Worms in a print-run of either three or six thousand. Copies of the book were smuggled into England in bales of cloth, but were searched out and destroyed by agents of Cardinal Wolsey. Consequently, only two textually complete copies of Tyndale's book survive today. This is the opening page of St John's Gospel from one of them.

British Library, Printed Books, C.188.a.17

In England, vernacular Bibles were licensed in the 1530s, and 1563 saw an act of parliament providing for a Welsh translation of the Bible and Book of Common Prayer by St David's Day, 1567. Able literary and theological scholars were available for this work, and the New Testament and Prayer Book, by William Salesbury, appeared in 1567, and the complete Bible, the work of William Morgan, Bishop of Llandaf and later St Asaph, in 1588. The title pages of both, from copies held in the National Library of Wales, are illustrated here. This Bible became the foundation of modern Welsh literature and played a vital part in the survival of the Welsh language.

National Library of Wales

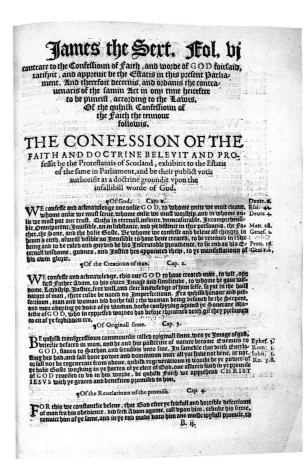

The influence of the continental Reformation was felt in Scotland from the 1520s. In 1557, a large group of noblemen took up arms against the French regent, Mary of Guise, in order to establish a reformed Church in Scotland. Two years later, the Calvinist John Knox returned from exile in Geneva and provided a focus for the reform movement. In 1560, the regent died during the siege of Leith, and peace was established by the Treaty of Edinburgh. In August, a parliament met which abolished papal jurisdiction, banned the mass and accepted a statement of ecclesiastical doctrine, known as the Confession of Faith, which had been drafted by Knox. The opening of the Confession of Faith is here shown in a contemporary book of acts of the Scottish parliament.

National Archives of Scotland GA1

Gloriana

Many of the figures who seem to embody the most epic qualities of the British national myth are women: Boadicea, Queen Elizabeth I and Queen Victoria spring to mind. Of these, Elizabeth is perhaps the most celebrated. Her long reign from 1558 to 1603 is often seen as a golden age of political, military and cultural achievement. However, the religious settlement imposed by Elizabeth and her ministers after the attempts of her sister Mary to reintroduce Catholicism was at first very fragile, and Elizabeth was at risk from Catholic conspiracies. Elizabeth became embroiled in a war against the massive Spanish empire which lasted much of her reign. Much of Elizabeth's reputation as 'Gloriana' reflects her own skill as a self-publicist, making use of such devices as the royal progress through a succession of country houses and semi-official but lavish celebrations of her accession day.

In about 1576, Henry Howard, a younger brother of the Duke of Norfolk, gave Elizabeth a manuscript containing a Latin eulogy of the queen written in his own hand. This portrait of Elizabeth formed the frontispiece of the manuscript. Howard's attempts to ingratiate himself with Elizabeth proved fruitless; she distrusted him, and suspected him of trying to win the hand of Mary Queen of Scots. Elizabeth's successor, James I, proved more responsive to Howard's flattery, and he became Earl of Northampton in 1604.
British Library, Egerton MS. 944, f. 1v

The failure of the 1588 Spanish armada, a huge fleet for the invasion of England, has been seen as a pivotal event in the history of Elizabeth's reign and in English popular history. In fact, however, the initial skirmishes between the English and Spanish fleets were inconclusive, and, as the Spanish fleet retreated northwards followed by the English, both sides suffered terrible losses as a result of bad weather, disease and shortage of supplies. These dramatic engravings by the Elizabethan cartographer Robert Adams show an engagement between the Spanish and English fleets.
British Library, G.929

Elizabeth's energetic involvement in government is shown by the frequency with which her characteristically bold and imposing signature appears on state papers of all kinds.
Public Record Office, SP 11/4 no. 2

[Manuscript image of Mary's handwritten letter in French, signed "Vostre tres affectionnee et bien bonne sœur MARIR"]

Robert Beale was an official of Queen Elizabeth's council. He carried the death warrant for Mary to Fotheringhay castle and read it aloud before the execution. His papers include sketches of the trial and execution of Mary. The first sketch shows Mary being brought before the commissioners assigned to try her. The second shows three different stages of the execution: Mary entering the hall; Mary attended by her women on the scaffold; and Mary lying at the block with the executioner's axe ready to strike.

British Library, Additional MS 48027, ff. 569*, 650*

Mary's last letter was written just six hours before her execution. It is in French and addressed to King Henri III of France, the younger brother of Mary's first husband, François I of France, who had died in 1560. Mary describes to Henri how, 'having...thrown myself into the power of the Queen my cousin, at whose hands I have suffered much for almost twenty years, I have finally been condemned to death by her and her Estates.' She declares that she scorns death and will 'meet it innocent of any crime'.

National Library of Scotland, Adv. MS 54.1.1

Mary, Queen of Scots reigned in Scotland for only six years, from 1561 to 1567. At first, despite some Protestant protests, Mary's insistence on following her Catholic beliefs did not create any major problems for her government. However, as a result of her successive marriages to Henry Stuart, Lord Darnley, and James Hepburn, Earl of Bothwell, antagonism towards Mary's religious beliefs increased, and she was forced to flee to England. Mary's cousin, Queen Elizabeth, was sympathetic to her plight, but, as a Catholic with a claim to the English throne, Mary was a potential focus for plots against Elizabeth, and Elizabeth confined Mary to prison and held her for nearly 20 years. Eventually, Mary was brought to trial for complicity in a conspiracy, and was finally executed on 8 February 1587 in Fotheringhay castle in Northamptonshire.

The Stuart Succession

James's eldest son was Henry Frederick, an intelligent, cultured and vigorous young man who admired Sir Walter Raleigh and took as a role model the learned soldier-poet Sir Philip Sidney. These are the letters by which in 1610 James in appointed Henry Prince of Wales and Earl of Chester. Henry tragically died of typhoid at the age of sixteen, so that his younger brother Charles eventually succeeded James.
British Library, Additional MS. 36932

Queen Elizabeth was very skilful in guarding her privacy, and the reasons for her refusal to marry or name a successor remain mysterious. Her obstinacy in this respect drove her courtiers to distraction. Her obvious successor was James VI of Scotland, the son of Mary Queen of Scots, who was a great-great grandson of Henry VII. During the 1590s, James unsuccessfully engaged in widespread intrigue to try and secure his succession. However, when Elizabeth eventually died in 1603, he became King James I of England without much fuss. James hoped to build on the union of the crowns of England and Scotland to achieve a fuller integration of law, government and religion, but failed to achieve this 'union of hearts and minds'. Instead he became notorious for elaborating in his book *Basilikon Doron* the concept of the divine right of kings, which helped create enormous divisions during the reign of his son Charles.

James VI saw his accession to the throne of England as an act of God. On 4 April 1603, he made this proclamation to the Scottish people, and on the following day he rode south to claim his kingdom. At the time, the Scots diarist Robert Birrel recorded the 'grate lamentatioun and mourning among the commons for the loss of thair daylie sicht of thair blessit prince'.
National Archives of Scotland, Register House series: RH14/3

43

William Shakespeare (1564–1616) is thought of as an enigmatic mysterious figure about whose life not much is known. As his plays became ever more celebrated for their insights into the human condition, the man himself became almost forgotten. But, in recent years, detailed research among the everyday historical documents in archives and record offices has revealed a great deal of information about Shakespeare the man: a Stratford visitor to London records conversations with him; Shakespeare makes depositions in court about his landlord; he forgets to pay his taxes; he gets involved in a violent quarrel on Bankside; Londoners record in their diaries visits to his plays. There is doubtless much more to be discovered. Of course, these archival gleanings tell us little about how Shakespeare became an incomparable national symbol. The story of this lies in the way subsequent generations viewed his plays, and their reinvention of Shakespeare as their view of his plays shifted. However, this rediscovery in the archives of Shakespeare the man perhaps gives a new dimension to his status as a national icon. They encourage a view of Shakespeare as a worldly-wise, down-to-earth and commonsensical observer of human affairs, which in many ways accords with one aspect of English self-perception.

In the late 1590s, Shakespeare was a member of a theatrical company which performed under the patronage of the Lord Chamberlain, an official of the royal household. When James I came to the throne, this company was taken under royal patronage, and as the King's Players became the leading troupe in the country. This warrant of 1603 is for the issue of royal letters authorising Shakespeare and his companions freely to perform plays of all types, not only in their usual house called the Globe, but also in all town halls, moot halls and other convenient places.
Public Record Office, C 82/1690 (78)

The diary of John Manningham, a law student in London from 1598–1605, gives an entertaining portrait of late Elizabethan London. He describes a performance of *Twelfth Night* at the Middle Temple in 1602. He also, in the entry shown here, dated 16 March 1602, recounts the following (probably apocryphal) anecdote about Shakespeare: 'Upon a tyme when Burbidge played Rich. 3 there was a citizen grene so farr in liking with him, that before shee went from the play she appointed him to come that night unto hir in the name of Ri: the 3. Shakespeare overhearing their conclusion went before, was intertained, and at his game ere Burbidge came. Then message being brought that Rich. the 3d was at the dore, Shakespeare caused returne to be made that William the Conqueror was before Rich. the 3.'
British Library, Harley MS. 5353, f. 29v

William Shakespeare

The opening pages of *Twelfth Night*, the play attended by Manningham in 1602, from the first collected edition of Shakespeare's works, the First Folio, published posthumously in 1623.

British Library C.39.k.15

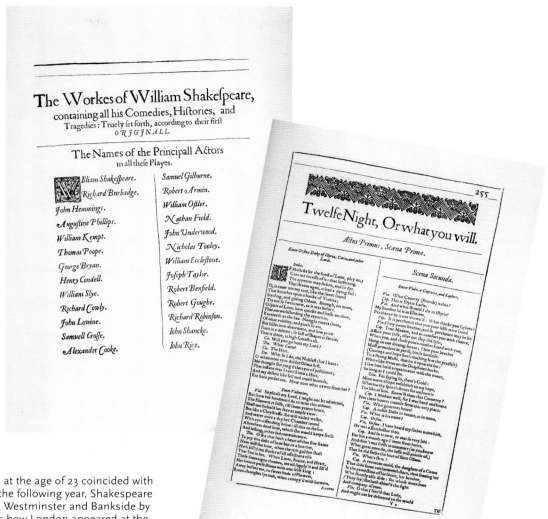

Shakespeare's departure from Stratford at the age of 23 coincided with that of a visiting company of actors. In the following year, Shakespeare settled in London. This view of London, Westminster and Bankside by the Cheshire artist William Smith shows how London appeared at the time of Shakespeare's arrival. The two famous Bankside theatres, the Rose and the Globe, where Shakespeare's plays were to be performed, had not yet been built, but they eventually occupied the site of the two circular bear-baiting enclosures shown in the foreground.

British Library, Sloane MS. 2596, f. 52

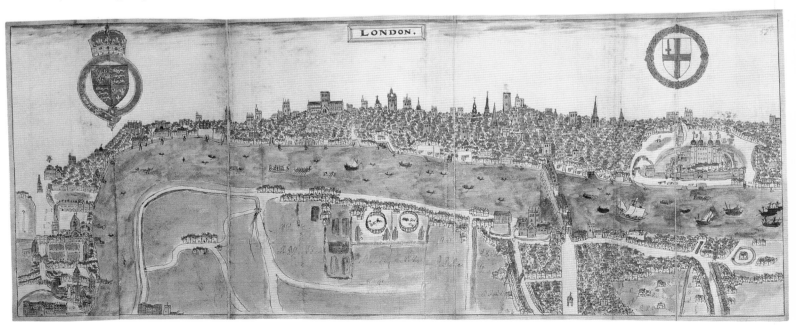

In 1584, during the reign of Elizabeth I, the Virgin Queen, Sir Walter Raleigh was granted the right to discover and colonise 'remote, heathen and barbarous lands', in North America, in the queen's name. His settlement at Roanoke Island (now in North Carolina) failed, but in 1606 King James I of England and VI of Scotland granted a similar charter to the Virginia Company of London. Three ships were dispatched from England in December 1606, carrying settlers under the leadership of Captain John Smith. In May 1607 they camped at Jamestown, where they encountered the native Powhatan tribe under the leadership of the powerful chieftain Wahunsonacock. During the sporadic warfare between the settlers and native Americans which followed, Matoaka, the daughter of Wahunsonacock, known to the English as Pocahontas, is said to have saved Captain Smith's life, and helped to bring about peace by converting to Christianity and marrying the colonist John Rolfe. She visited England with her husband in 1617 and was presented at Court, but died on her way home and was buried at Gravesend, Kent. Rolfe returned to Virginia, to continue cultivating the tobacco he had first introduced in 1614, thereby securing the long-term prosperity of the young colony.

This early map of Virginia, engraved for John Smith by William Hole in 1608, shows details of the newly discovered lands around the settlement of Jamestown. Shown also are the names of the native American peoples encountered by the settlers and depictions of Pocahontas (at top right) and her father (top left).

Public Record Office, MPG 1/284

Virginia: An Early American Colony

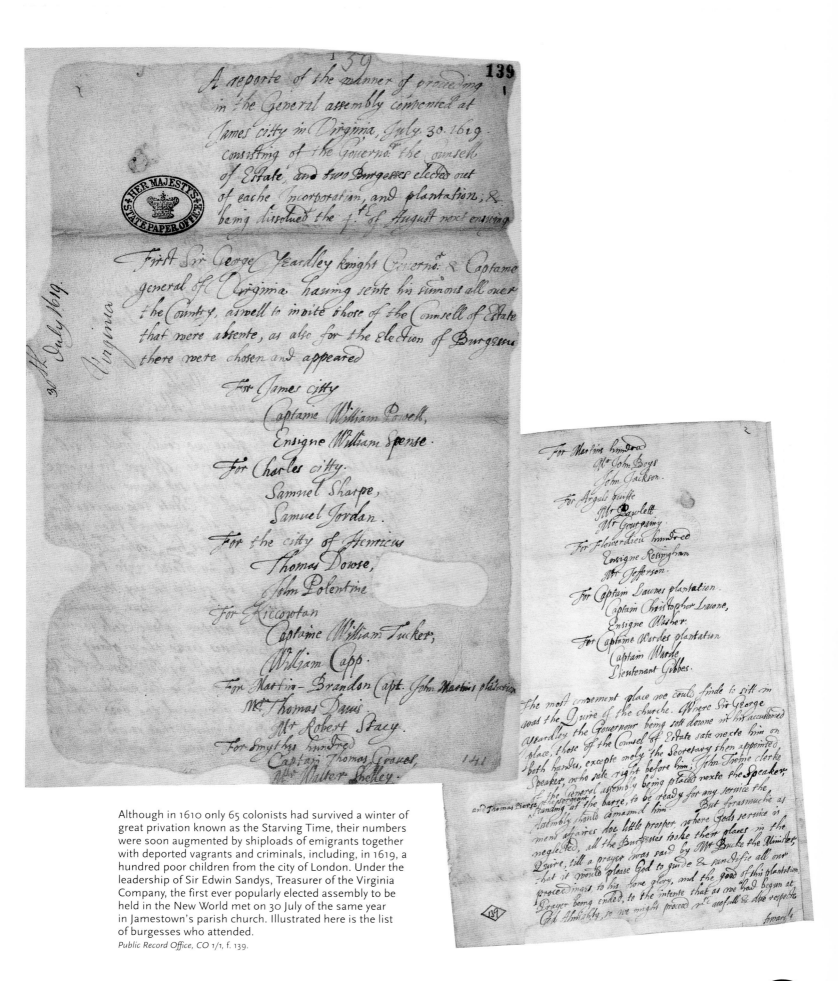

Although in 1610 only 65 colonists had survived a winter of great privation known as the Starving Time, their numbers were soon augmented by shiploads of emigrants together with deported vagrants and criminals, including, in 1619, a hundred poor children from the city of London. Under the leadership of Sir Edwin Sandys, Treasurer of the Virginia Company, the first ever popularly elected assembly to be held in the New World met on 30 July of the same year in Jamestown's parish church. Illustrated here is the list of burgesses who attended.

Public Record Office, CO 1/1, f. 139.

On 26 October 1605 the Catholic peer Lord Mounteagle, recently arrived at his house in Hoxton, London in preparation for the opening session of parliament on 5 November, received an anonymous letter warning him not on any account to attend the house, which would receive a 'terrible blow'. Rumours of Catholic plots against the staunchly Protestant King James were rife, and when Mounteagle immediately informed Robert Cecil, Earl of Salisbury, the king's Chief Secretary, of the threat, Cecil's reaction was at first to discount it. However at the king's urging on the evening of 4 November a search was undertaken of the cellars beneath the House of Lords. This was followed by a midnight raid revealing 36 barrels of gunpowder under the supervision of 'a tall and desperate fellow', carrying a watch and matches about his person, who named himself as John Johnson. Later identified as Guy Fawkes, a staunch Catholic, he admitted that he had intended to blow up the Upper House.

The discovery was noted briefly in the margin of the House of Commons Journals: 'one Johnston, servant to Mr Thomas Percye was there apprehended who had placed 36 barrells of gunpowder in the vawt'. Because virtually all the Commons records were destroyed by fire in 1834 this is the one surviving reference amongst the archives of Parliament.
House of Lords Record Office, House of Commons MS Journal, 5 November 1605

The king himself drew up instructions for questioning the prisoner, including the use of torture. Within four days the royal commissioners had elicited the information that his name was Guy Fawkes and that his fellow plotters were important Catholic gentry including Thomas Percy and Robert Catseby. Their purpose was to blow up the king and nobles and replace James with his daughter Princess Elizabeth. Much of this information appeared in Fawkes's first confession dated 9 November: the faintness of the signature suggests the use of torture.
Public Record Office, SP 14/216, no 54

Guy Fawkes's second confession, dated 17 November, was a fuller version of the first, embellished for dramatic effect, and giving far fuller details about the plot which was intended to lead to a full-scale rebellion. This time the signature (above) was clear and strong.
Public Record Office, SP 14/216, no 101

Gunpowder, Treason and Plot

But there was to be no escape for Guy Fawkes and his fellow-conspirators – tried for and convicted of treason, they were executed on 30–31 January 1606, some near St Paul's Cathedral, others, including Fawkes himself, beside the Houses of Parliament. Although the plot was itself only one of many threats to Stuart Britain, the many unanswered questions remaining after the trial fuelled speculation that it had represented a major and profound Catholic threat. Popular celebrations of the event merged with, and in the end took over, older rituals of fire marking the onset of winter and the Fifth of November is one of the very few non-ecclesiastical festivals to survive into modern times. Firework displays were already a popular event in the early seventeeth century, as is shown by this colourful depiction of the celebrations of the marriage of James I's daughter, Princess Elizabeth, in 1613.

British Library, Royal MS 17.C. xxxv, f. 6v

The initial experiences of King Charles I as a ruler were frustrating. Parliament refused to grant him taxes, was suspicious of his religious views, and sought to circumscribe his power. From 1629, Charles tried to rule without parliament, but in 1640 was forced to recall parliament and make substantial concessions to it. Charles then awkwardly attempted to recover the ground he had lost. Following disputes over the control of an army against rebels in Ireland, Charles raised his standard against his opponents at Nottingham in 1642, marking the beginning of civil war. By 1646, he had been defeated by the forces of the Westminster parliament, and became their prisoner. Attempts to reach a political settlement proved abortive and there was a further outbreak of fighting. Charles was finally tried and executed in 1649.

This portrait of Charles is painted on the cover of a roll recording the proceedings of the Court of King's Bench, which heard many of the most important criminal cases.
Public Record Office, KB 27/1681

In 1641, Charles ordered five members of parliament and one member of the House of Lords to be arrested and tried for treason. These are his instructions to the attorney-general for the proceedings. In the third paragraph, the name of Lord Kimbolton has been deleted from the list of witnesses for the trial, because Charles decided to prosecute him instead. In the first line of the document, the number of men to be arrested has been accordingly altered from five to six. The members were warned that Charles intended to arrest them and escaped. All that Charles's action achieved was to alienate moderates, who were horrified by this violation of parliamentary jurisdiction.
British Library, Egerton MS. 2546, f. 20

Charles I

In March 1645, King Charles's son, Prince Charles, then just twelve years old, went to take command of the royalist forces in the south-west and said farewell to his father for the last time. By July 1645, King Charles was a fugitive in Wales, and on 5 August he sent this letter to his son, urging him whenever he found himself in personal danger to flee to France and to place himself under the care of his mother. However, a number of influential royalists were doubtful whether the prince should yet leave the country, and it was not until March 1646 that he finally went to France.

British Library, Harley MS. 6988, f. 185

On 1 January 1649, the House of Commons declared that Charles had committed treason by levying war against the parliament and the kingdom of England. On 6 January, the Commons established themselves as the sole court for the king's trial. On 20 January, Charles was brought into Westminster Hall to be tried. He refused to acknowledge the legality of the court and on 27 January he was condemned to death. This is his death warrant. It is signed by 59 people. The first signature is that of John Bradshaw, who presided over the trial; the third signature is that of Oliver Cromwell. The warrant says that the king is to be put to death 'by the severing of his head from his body'. Charles was executed in front of the Banqueting House at Whitehall on 30 January.

House of Lords Record Office

The term 'cavalier' used for the royalist soldiers during the English civil war was at first a term of abuse. It was derived from 'cavellero', a term for a knightly horseman, and was meant to imply that the royalists were just play-acting at being soldiers. However, the royalists came to like the suggestion of dashing gallantry implied in this name, and adopted the term. The first usage of the phrase 'roundhead' for the parliamentary soldiers dates from 1641, and is said to have referred to a severe puritan haircut.

Some banners of the parliamentary army.
British Library, Additional MS. 12447, ff. 23v, 24

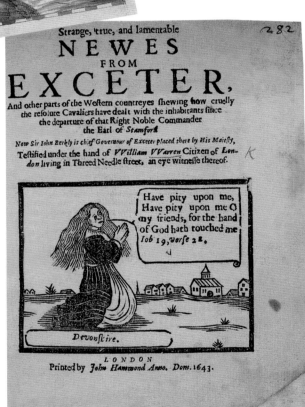

Richard Symonds (b. 1617) escaped from prison to join the royalist army, and became a member of the king's lifeguards. Between 1643–5 he followed the king all over the country, taking part in many of the most critical engagements of the civil war. He kept a diary of the journeys of the royal army between 1644–1646. Symonds was an enthusiastic amateur archaeologist, and his diary mixes antiquarian jottings on churches and historic buildings visited by him with reports of military engagements. On the left-hand page of these entries for July 1643, Symonds describes a visit to the church of Sapperton in Gloucestershire; on the right-hand page, he notes how two foot soldiers were hanged on trees in the hedgerow for pillaging country villages.
British Library, Additional MS. 17062, ff. 43v-44

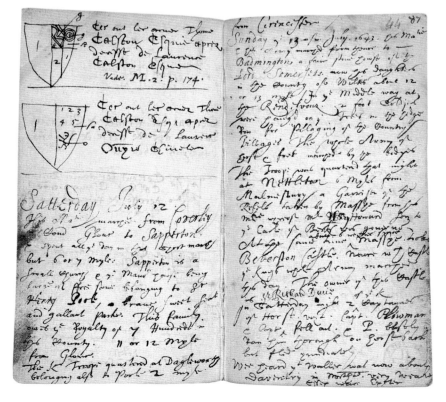

In 1640, George Thomason (d. 1666), a London bookseller, recognising that a major political crisis was developing and wishing to make a record of it, began systematically to collect all the books and pamphlets he could lay his hands on. During the next twenty years, he acquired more than 22,000 items. His collection, now in the British Library, provides a remarkable record of the ideological cross-currents of the period of the civil war and commonwealth. Among the many rare items in the Thomason Tracts is the above pamphlet describing alleged atrocities committed in 1643 by royalist forces at Exeter, Bristol and Cirencester, where it was alleged that inhabitants of the town had been forced to spend a night standing naked in a pond by royalist soldiers, who had called them 'Roundheaded Citizens, Parliament Rogues, and Parliament Dogs'.
British Library, E.70.(13.)

The Commonwealth and the Lord Protector

Charles I, like his predecessors, had used a great seal showing, on one side, the monarch enthroned in splendour with orb and sceptre and on the other, the king in armour riding a horse. Following the execution of Charles I, the design of the great seal was altered to reflect the new political circumstances. On one side was a carefully engraved map of Britain; on the other a picture of the House of Commons in session. This is a proof impression of the second version of this seal, which was first used in 1651. The legend reads 'IN THE THIRD YEARE OF FREEDOME BY GODS BLESSING RESTORED 1651'.

British Library, Detached Seal, xxxiv.17

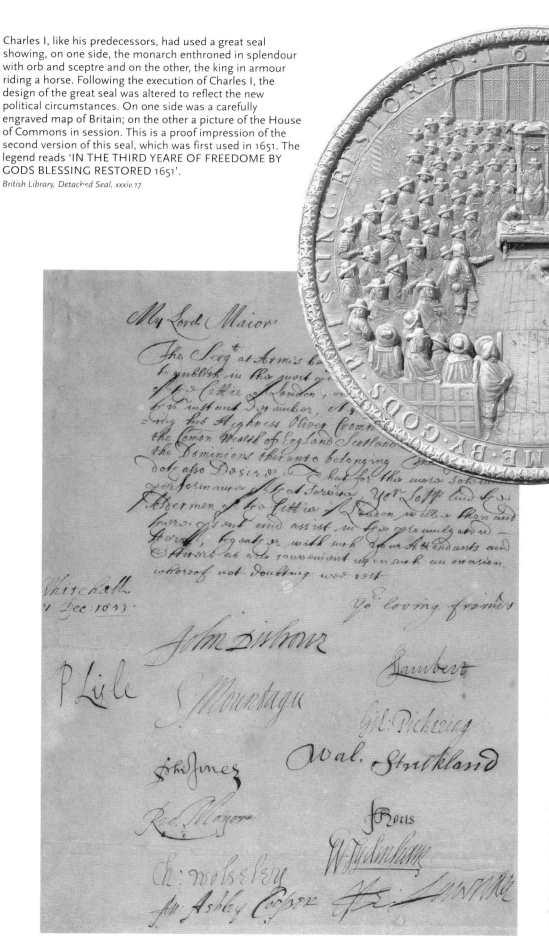

Oliver Cromwell (1599–1658), a member of the Huntingdonshire gentry, emerged as the most powerful of the parliamentary military commanders after his victories at Marston Moor and Naseby. He took a leading part in the trial and execution of Charles I, then during 1650–1 overcame the threats to the English parliament offered by first the Irish and then the Scots. However, there were increasing conflicts between parliament and the army as to the future shape of the constitution, with the army forcibly suspending the sitting of parliament. Eventually, Cromwell came to the conclusion that he should assume supreme power. He refused the title of King, but instead on 16 December 1653 was installed as Protector. This is the order of the council of state, an executive body set up after Charles's execution, for the proclamation of Cromwell as Protector. After Cromwell's death, his son Richard succeeded him in this title, but, lacking his father's gift and force of character, his regime quickly collapsed.

British Library, Additional MS. 18739, f. 1

On the execution of Charles I in 1649 his son Charles was proclaimed Charles II in Scotland, but despite putting up a brave resistance he and his supporters were defeated at the battle of Worcester in 1651. After 40 days in hiding, Charles managed, narrowly, to escape to France where he endured an impoverished exile. Political and military turmoil followed the death of Oliver Cromwell in September 1658 but from it emerged the powerful figure of General Monk, one of Cromwell's generals with a strong base in Scotland. Monk was receptive to a growing desire in England for establishing the legitimate authority of a newly-elected parliament – and ultimately agreed to the return of the monarchy itself. By the Spring of 1659 negotiations were under way with the exiled king.

The Declaration of Breda, of 4 April 1660, marked Charles's intention to return to his kingdom. An open letter to all his subjects, drafted with the help of his adviser Edward Hyde, it announced his desire to bring to an end all the recent discord and to establish peace and harmony. For his own part he hoped for a general amnesty, a settlement of land disputes, the issuing of back pay to the army, and for liberty of conscience, but the terms of these he would leave to a free parliament.
Public Record Office, SP 18/221, no 4 (iii).

The Speaker, Sir Harbottle Grimston, replied in fulsome tones in May 1660, congratulating Charles on his conquest by patience of the nation, and begging him to reign as King over peoples' hearts.
Public Record Office, SP 29/1

The famous medallist and seal engraver Thomas Simon had produced coins and seals for Cromwell. After the Restoration, he was supplanted by a royalist, but petitioned Charles II for work. Charles was impressed, and Simon was eventually reinstated as the chief designer of coins and seals. The reasons for Charles's enthusiasm are apparent from this superb design for a great seal for the king included in this warrant of 1662 authorising the making of the seal.
British Library, Additional MS. 71450

The Great Fire of London

At the time of the restoration of the monarchy in 1660, the city of London still essentially retained its medieval shape, with many ancient buildings, chiefly of wood, crowded in narrow lanes. On 2 September 1666, a fire broke out on the premises of Thomas Farrinor, the king's baker, which rapidly spread to adjoining properties. The fire lasted until 6 September, and destroyed nearly two-thirds of the city. The area of devastation covered 436 acres containing more than 400 streets and over 13,000 houses. Among the prestigious buildings that were destroyed were St Paul's cathedral, the Guildhall, the Royal Exchange, the Customs House, Newgate and Fleet Prisons, 44 halls of livery companies and 89 parish churches. The total value of property destroyed was reckoned at more than ten million pounds, but only six people died. The disaster caught the imagination of Europe. The French viewed it as a judgement on the English for beheading their King; the Dutch, at that time at war with England, considered it a rightful punishment of their enemy. In England, false rumours ascribed the fire to Catholic agents, a charge which was enshrined in the inscription on the monument built by Sir Christopher Wren to commemorate the fire.

This map shows the streets and lanes of the city which were affected by the fire. It was made in December 1666 by John Leeke at the order of the Mayor and Aldermen of the city. Although Wren and others prepared grandiose schemes for rebuilding the city, the old street pattern was retained. New building regulations were, however, introduced to reduce the risk of another fire.
British Library, Additional MS. 5415 E

The Hearth Tax was a duty on each fireplace in use in every house, and was levied from 1662–6 and 1679–74. The collector of the tax for the area of London which included Pudding Lane had only begun surveying the houses in his neighbourhood in August 1666, and his record of Pudding Lane was probably made only a few days before the fire broke out. The entry for Thomas Farrinor (the ninth entry on the right hand page) records that he had five hearths and one oven, presumably the oven in which the fire broke out.
Public Record Office, E 179/252/32

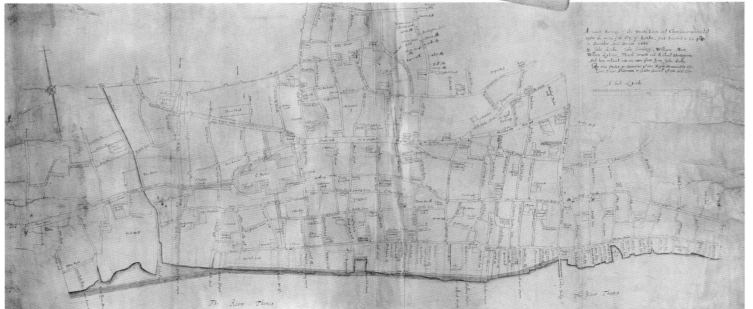

Charles II's brother, James, Duke of York, had become a Catholic by 1671, and his conversion soon became widely known. Attempts were made to ensure that he would not become king, but he nevertheless succeeded to the throne as James II in 1685. He then completely overplayed his hand, promoting Catholics to key positions and seeking to overturn restrictions on them. The birth of a son to James and his wife raised the spectre of a Catholic royal dynasty, and opposition leaders invited Prince William of Orange, the husband of James's sister Mary, to invade. William landed in Torbay on 5 November 1688. James considered battle but lost his nerve, and eventually fled to France. William and Mary

Portrait of James II from the Guild Book of the Barber Surgeons of York. This volume was begun in the middle ages and continued in use to record proceedings of the guild until the end of the 18th century. At the beginning of each reign, a portrait of the new monarch was inserted in the book.
British Library, Egerton MS. 2572, f. 15

When parliament offered William and Mary the throne in February 1689, they accompanied their offer with a Declaration of Rights, the first page of which is shown here. The text was written first in the Commons; the amendments were made in the House of Lords, and recorded by a clerk who also presumably made the large ink blot. The Declaration stated that parliaments should be held frequently; that elections should be free; that freedom of speech should be preserved; and that parliamentary consent was required for taxation, the suspension of statutes and the maintenance of a standing army. The Declaration formed the basis of the Bill of Rights, enacted in December 1689, which has been described as 'next to Magna Carta the greatest landmark in the constitution of England and the nearest approach to the written constitutions of other countries'.
House of Lords Record Office T/6

The Glorious Revolution

were offered the crown of England as joint monarchs in February 1689 and the crown of Scotland shortly afterwards. There was still support for James in Ireland, and the hold of William and Mary on their new dominions was only finally secured when William defeated James at the Battle of the Boyne in 1690.

Portrait of William and Mary from the Guild Book of the Barber Surgeons of York.
British Library, Egerton MS. 2572, f. 16

On 4 April 1689 the Scottish Convention of Estates declared in the Claim of Right that James had forfeited his right to rule by invading 'the fundamental constitution of this Kingdom and altering it from a legal limited monarchy to an arbitrary despotic power'. A week later William and Mary were proclaimed King and Queen of Scotland.
National Archives of Scotland, Register House proclamations: RH14/288

Sir Christopher Wren and St Paul's Cathedral

Known best for his remarkable transformation of London in the aftermath of the Great Fire, Sir Christopher Wren (1632-1723) was a polymath who in his later life was often heard to express regrets that he had never continued with an early interest in medicine. Fascinated by mathematics and inventions, and a founder member of the Royal Society, he became a professor of astronomy at Oxford at the age of 25. Here he produced important work on Saturn and its rings, comets and eclipses while designing buildings, including the Sheldonian Theatre, as a sideline. But after a visit to the French Court at Paris and Versailles in 1665 he became increasingly interested in architecture, developed plans for replanning and rebuilding London, and became Surveyor-General of the King's Works in 1669 – a post he held for half a century, until 1718, serving five sovereigns. Apart from St Paul's Cathedral, arguably his masterpiece (and where he was to be buried in 1723), his best-known buildings are some 60 London churches including St Stephen's Walbrook and St Bride's Fleet Street; the Library of Trinity College Cambridge; parts of the royal palaces at Hampton Court and Kensington; the Royal Hospital at Chelsea;

and the Royal Naval College at Greenwich. A contemporary eulogised him as 'a benefactor to mankind and an ornament to the age in which he lived'.

Work began on St Paul's Cathedral in 1675 but it was not formally completed until 1710. Wren's own wish was for a domed building based on a Greek cross with arms of equal length – as exemplified by the Great Model he produced in 1673, whereas the Church authorities favoured the Latin cross, closer to the traditional layout of the medieval cathedral with its elongated nave. Such opposing views produced tensions and resulted in an evolutionary approach to the design of the cathedral throughout the 35 years of its construction.

This engraving of a Wren design for the north elevation was made in 1702, when the designs for the dome, Wren's crowning achievement, were moving towards their final form – although considerable changes were to be made to the west towers as finally built.
Public Record Office, Work 38/165

In reaction to a plot to assassinate King William III in 1696, parliament established an association for the defence of the king to which all office holders were obliged to subscribe. This oath roll has the signatures of officers and others who were working on the rebuilding of St Paul's cathedral, including those of Wren himself and Grinling Gibbons.
Public Record Office, C213/397

The 18th and 19th Centuries

Tell me the auld, auld story
O' hoo the Union brocht
Puir Scotland into being
As a country worth a thocht.

Hugh McDiarmid, *The Parrot Cry*

With the overthrow of James II, the Stuarts became exiles in France, where it was hoped that they might one day prove to be the means by which Britain was returned to the Catholic fold. An Act of Succession passed before the death of William III declared that the monarch must be a Protestant, and James's Protestant daughter Anne succeeded William. Anne had no heir and, in order to ensure a Protestant succession, the English parliament decided that the next king should be a German prince, George, the Elector of Hanover. The Scottish parliament resented the way in which the Hanoverian succession had been handled and threatened to choose its own king. In 1707, the Scottish parliament was abolished and an Act of Union between the two countries was passed. The Stuarts still hoped for support in Scotland, and made periodic unsuccessful landings there. In 1745, the Stuart claimant Charles Edward Stuart, 'The Young Pretender', invaded Scotland and attracted substantial support in the Highlands. His force penetrated as far south as Derby, but was eventually forced back north and massacred at the battle of Culloden.

Interior of a tavern at Woolwich in Kent, drawn by George Scharf in 1826.
British Library, Additional MS. 36489, f.28

The defeat of the 1745 rising by both Lowland Scots and English helped forge a greater sense of common identity between them, albeit at the expense of the Highland Scots. The second half of the 18th century was characterised by a vibrant new sense of British identity, which was reinforced by victories over France and the acquisition of new colonies during the Seven Years' War of 1756 to 1763. National self-confidence was further bolstered by growing prosperity as a result of increasing industrialisation, growth in international trade and improvements in agricultural techniques. This new sense of British self-esteem was dented by the loss of the thirteen American colonies as a result of the American War of Independence, but almost immediately Europe was thrown into turmoil by the French Revolution and Britain became embroiled in a war with France which lasted, with short breaks, from 1793 to 1815. The wars against France reinforced the complex process by which Britain increasingly defined itself by its otherness from France and indeed the rest of Europe: as a Protestant, tenacious, pragmatic, conservative but liberty-loving people.

The Great Exhibition of 1851 sought to provide a massive demonstration of Britain's position as the richest and most powerful country in the world. However, 19th-century Britain was marked by many contradictions. The Industrial Revolution had made Britain very wealthy, but its new towns and cities were characterised by great poverty and squalor, and many foreign observers were convinced that revolution was inevitable. Britain ruled the largest empire the world had ever seen, but the administration of the empire was for much of the 19th century very loose-knit, with the most important possession, India, being controlled until 1857 by the archaic mechanism of the East India Company. Britain was immensely proud of its parliamentary democracy, but throughout the 19th century there was constant agitation for the reform of parliament and the extension of the right to vote. It is appropriate that the presiding literary genius of Victorian Britain was Charles Dickens, with his nostalgic longing for the days of posthorns and coaches on the one hand and his concern with social conditions on the other.

As the 19th century proceeded, the fissure lines within Britain became more evident again. The Scots and Welsh had been prominent in building the Empire, but at home they increasingly demanded greater autonomy. This was particularly marked in Wales, where the growth of nonconformity led to vehement demands for the disestablishment of the Church. As the 19th century closed, leading politicians were talking of the desirability of 'Home Rule All Round'.

By the beginning of the 18th century relations between Scotland and England, never easy bed-fellows, had grown very sour. Contributing factors were the deepening commercial crisis in Scotland, the massacre of members of the MacDonald clan in Glencoe in 1692 but more crucially, the failure of the Scots to establish their own trading colony on the isthmus of Panama. Almost one quarter of Scotland's liquid capital was sunk into the Company of Scotland to set up a colony at Darien, but the venture was ill-conceived and doomed to failure. The Scots laid the blame squarely at the feet of King William, who had instructed the English colonists not to help them, and the English who, fearful for their trading privileges, had opposed the project.

The situation deteriorated further over the vexed question of who should inherit the throne on the death of Queen Anne. The English parliament was desperate to secure a Protestant and not a Jacobite heir

and passed an Act settling the succession on James I and VI's Hanoverian descendants, without consulting the Scots. In retaliation the Scottish parliament passed the Act of Security in 1704, stating that unless they were granted free trade, the Scottish crown would pass to a person of their own choosing. England hit back with an Alien Act banning Scottish imports and treating all Scots in England as aliens until negotiations for a full union were begun or Scotland accepted the Hanoverian succession.

Talks between the two countries commenced in April 1706 and by July the 25 articles of union were agreed by both sides. In Scotland the act was pushed through parliament with the help of £20 000 liberally dispensed in bribes and government propaganda from the pen of Daniel Defoe. Many ordinary Scots opposed the union, fearing that the incorporating union proposed would mean Scotland's absorption into England. There were riots in Glasgow and Stirling and troops were brought in to Edinburgh to maintain order.

1 May 1707 was the first day of the Union. England and Scotland were henceforth joined together as Great Britain under one united parliament. Each country kept its own legal system and established Church, but weights, measures, coinage, and customs and excise were standardised. Scottish merchants gained freedom of trade and to compensate Scotland for taking on a share of England's national debt a sum of nearly £400 000, known as the Equivalent, was paid out to compensate Darien shareholders. Reaction to the Union was enthusiastic in England but on 1 May in Edinburgh the church bells rang out the tune 'Why should I be sad on my wedding day'.

In a letter to the Secretary of State, the Earl of Mar, in favour of an incorporating Union rather than a federal one, the pro-Union Earl of Cromartie comments: 'Unless wee be a part each of other, the Union will be as a blood puddin to bind a Catt...May wee be Brittains and down goe the old ignominious names of Scotland, of England...'
National Archives of Scotland, RH14/288

The Union of 1707

This petition from the royal burgh of Stirling, one of 97 anti-Union addresses sent to the Scottish Parliament, expresses the fear of many Scots that the Union would bring with it an increasing burden of taxation, November 1706.

National Archives of Scotland, Parliamentary records: PA7/28/48

The Exemplification of the Articles of Union, an official copy of the act passed through the English Parliament, features the portrait of Queen Anne.

National Archives of Scotland, State Papers: SP13/10

The term Prime Minister began to be used in the early years of the 18th century, but it was Sir Robert Walpole (1676–1745) who first used the powers of patronage and financial control associated with the position of First Lord of the Treasury to maintain a tight grip on the day-to-day business of government and ensure his own political dominance. Prime Ministers ever since have held the official position of First Lord of the Treasury, although nowadays this is a nominal title. Walpole's skilful use of political patronage led to many complaints that he was running a corrupt 'Robinocracy'. Typical of the satirical jibes directed at him is this poem by Jonathan Swift, the author of *Gulliver's Travels*, which accuses Walpole of 'selling his Country to purchase his peace' and denounces him as 'the Cur dog of Brittain & spaniel of Spain'.

British Library, Additional MS. 22625, f. 26

The land on which Downing Street stands was acquired in 1651 by Sir George Downing, who was raised in New England and was one of the first graduates of Harvard University. In the 1680s, Downing redeveloped his land in Whitehall to form Downing Street, and in 1732 George II gave Walpole the house which is now 10 Downing Street as a perquisite of the office of First Lord of the Treasury. Walpole first occupied the house in 1735, following extensive renovations. No. 10 became established as the usual official residence of the Prime Minister during the early 19th century. This view of Downing Street in 1827 was made by John Chessell Buckler, who unsuccessfully entered the competition to build the Houses of Parliament.

British Museum, Department of Prints and Drawings, Crace Collection, portfolio xvi, no. 65

Hallelujah Handel

Handel is considered a quintessentially English composer – Berlioz complained that his music was like 'a tub of pork and beer'. However, he was born Georg Friederich Händel at Halle in Germany in 1685, and made his early reputation in Italy. He was appointed *kapellmeister* to the Elector of Hanover in 1710, but was given permission to work in London, where his music celebrating the Treaty of Utrecht attracted royal attention, and he was given a pension by Queen Anne. Following Anne's death in 1714, the Elector of Hanover became King of England; Handel's pension was doubled and he became teacher of music to the king's children. Handel first became well known in England with his Italian operas, but in the 1730s he introduced the oratorio – a setting of sacred text using the dramatic and musical structure of opera – to England, and thereafter made most of his money from works of this type. Handel was also a prolific composer of music for state occasions, such as the *Water Music*, composed for a serenade on the Thames in about 1717, and the *Music for the Royal Fireworks*, written for the celebrations of the Treaty of Aix-la-Chapelle in 1749 (and composed for an orchestra without violins, at the king's special request). Unusually for a composer at this time, Handel's work continued to be performed and revered in England after his death in 1759, a series of annual commemoration concerts at Westminster Abbey being inaugurated on the 25th anniversary of his death in 1784.

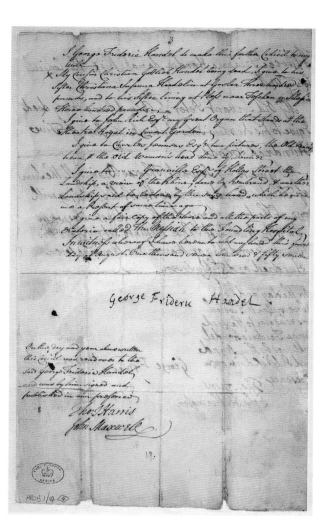

On 6 April 1759, Handel, already blind and very ill, collapsed during a performance of *Messiah*. On 11 April he dictated an amendment to his will; on 14 April he died. This is Handel's will. He left his music books, harpsichord and small organ to the musician John Christopher Smith, whose son afterwards gave the scores to George III. In 1957, Queen Elizabeth II gave these manuscripts, together with the rest of the Royal Music Library, to the British Library, where they form the single largest collection of original manuscripts of any great composer.
Public Record Office, PROB 1/14

Handel's most famous oratorio was *Messiah*, written in just over three weeks in 1741. This is Handel's autograph manuscript of the most famous chorus from *Messiah*, the Hallelujah chorus. Although oratorios were settings of sacred texts, they used the musical structure of operas and were written for performance in the theatre. *Messiah* was first performed at a hall in Fishamble Street in Dublin in 1742. Its great popularity was largely due to a series of London performances given in aid of the Foundling Hospital, a refuge for abandoned children, in the 1750s. Handel is said to have remarked on composing the Hallelujah chorus, 'Whether I was in my body or out of my body as I wrote it I know not. God knows'.
British Library, RM 20.f.2, f. 103v

The final attempt to restore the Stuart dynasty to the British throne was led by James VII and I's grandson, the young and debonair Prince Charles Edward Stuart, known as the Young Pretender or more popularly, Bonnie Prince Charlie. Previous Jacobite risings in 1708 and 1715, led by his father James Edward Stuart and encouraged by the French, had failed through a combination of ill-luck and poor leadership.

Charles landed at Moidart on the west coast of Scotland in July 1745. He brought none of the French military support his Jacobite supporters had anticipated but after Cameron of Lochiel pledged his support, other clan chiefs and their men flocked to his standard. The Highland army swept south and in September descended on Edinburgh. Shortly afterwards the Jacobites secured a major victory at Prestonpans, defeating the only government army in Scotland. Buoyed by their success, Charles and his army marched into England and, encountering little resistance, penetrated as far south as Derby. When French military support failed to materialise and unaware of the movements of English Jacobites in the south, Charles' council of war took the decision to retreat north. The Jacobite army defeated government troops at Falkirk but once again

'A Scotch Highlander armed'.
British Library, Additional MS. 5253, f. 5

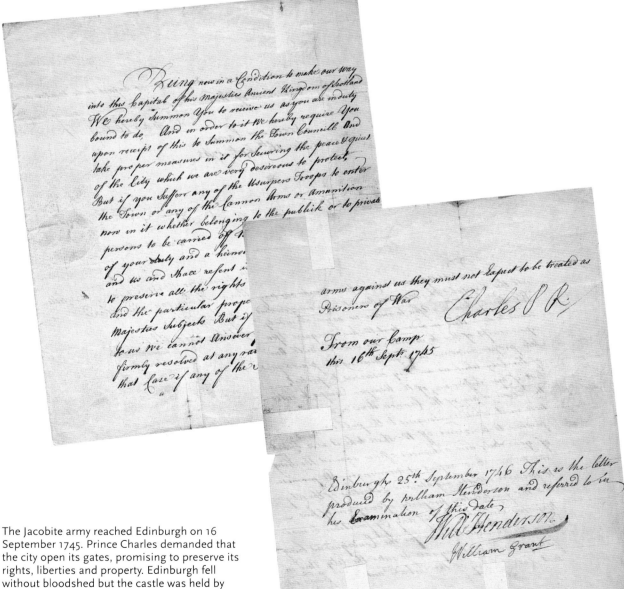

The Jacobite army reached Edinburgh on 16 September 1745. Prince Charles demanded that the city open its gates, promising to preserve its rights, liberties and property. Edinburgh fell without bloodshed but the castle was held by government forces.
National Archives of Scotland, High Court of Justiciary papers: JC26/135/2355

Bonnie Prince Charlie

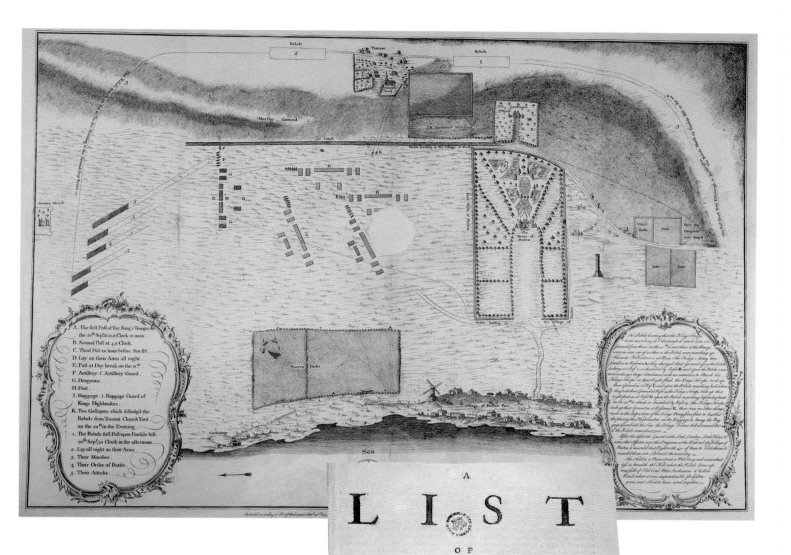

the clan chiefs persuaded the prince to draw back further into the Highlands. An exhausted and starving Jacobite army met the Duke of Cumberland's troops at Culloden outside Inverness in April 1746. Outnumbered and outmanoeuvred, they were heavily defeated, the survivors pursued and slaughtered with such vigour that Cumberland was nicknamed the 'butcher'.

The prince escaped to spend the next five months roaming the Highlands with £30 000 on his head, trying to elude search parties as he waited for a boat to take him back to France, most famously dressing up as Flora MacDonald's maid. A legend was being created, subsequently celebrated in poetry and song. Meanwhile the British government took revenge on his followers, proscribing tartan, highland dress and the carrying of arms, destroying the Highland culture in the process.

A plan of the battle of Prestonpans on 21 September 1745 where Sir John Cope's force succumbed to the ferocity of the Highlanders' charge and lost the battle within ten minutes.
National Archives of Scotland, Register House Plans: RHP93363

A list of some of the nearly 3,500 Jacobites judged guilty of treason includes leaders of the rebellion, tried and executed in London, and many ordinary soldiers who were transported or banished to the colonies.
National Archives of Scotland: Forfeited Estates papers: E706/2/5

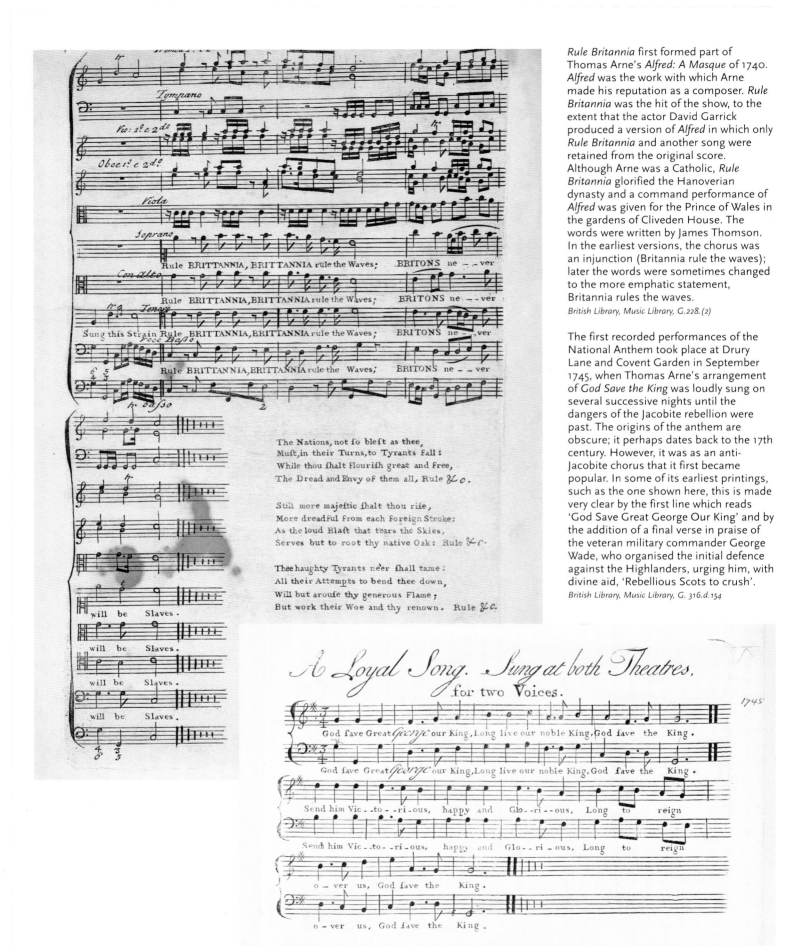

Rule Britannia first formed part of Thomas Arne's *Alfred: A Masque* of 1740. *Alfred* was the work with which Arne made his reputation as a composer. *Rule Britannia* was the hit of the show, to the extent that the actor David Garrick produced a version of *Alfred* in which only *Rule Britannia* and another song were retained from the original score. Although Arne was a Catholic, *Rule Britannia* glorified the Hanoverian dynasty and a command performance of *Alfred* was given for the Prince of Wales in the gardens of Cliveden House. The words were written by James Thomson. In the earliest versions, the chorus was an injunction (Britannia rule the waves); later the words were sometimes changed to the more emphatic statement, Britannia rules the waves.

British Library, Music Library, G.228.(2)

The first recorded performances of the National Anthem took place at Drury Lane and Covent Garden in September 1745, when Thomas Arne's arrangement of *God Save the King* was loudly sung on several successive nights until the dangers of the Jacobite rebellion were past. The origins of the anthem are obscure; it perhaps dates back to the 17th century. However, it was as an anti-Jacobite chorus that it first became popular. In some of its earliest printings, such as the one shown here, this is made very clear by the first line which reads 'God Save Great George Our King' and by the addition of a final verse in praise of the veteran military commander George Wade, who organised the initial defence against the Highlanders, urging him, with divine aid, 'Rebellious Scots to crush'.

British Library, Music Library, G. 316.d.154

A Passage to India

The East India Company was founded in 1600 to promote European trade in the exotic goods of the East. At first, there was not much demand for British goods in India, but during the 18th century Indian demand for British woollens and metalwares increased. As the Mughal Empire disintegrated, the power of the East India Company increased, and it began to acquire jurisdictional rights in Indian states beyond its three trading bases of Bombay, Madras and Calcutta. Company administrators such as Robert Clive and Warren Hastings substantially increased British power in India, but the large fortunes they acquired created suspicion of their activities at home. Regulation of the Company's activities in India was tightened up, with the creation of the post of governor-general in 1773 and the establishment of a board of control in 1784. Indian states continued to become clients of the British, and by the end of the Napoleonic wars British rule extended over considerable parts of the sub-continent. Policies of Anglicisation began to be implemented, with major changes to the legal and educational systems and campaigns against practices such as the burning of widows on the funeral pyres of their husbands. Westernising policies led to the Indian mutiny in 1857, after which the East India Company was disbanded

Resentment of the East India Company's monopoly of English trade with India led to the creation in 1698 of a rival 'English Company Trading to the East Indies'. This is the herald's letter by which the new company received its coat of arms, which is shown in the top left hand corner. Competition benefited neither company, and in 1702 they began to cooperate under a joint court of managers, finally amalgamating in 1709. The arms granted in this letter to the 'New Company' became those of the United East India Company', which were familiar on flags, ships and documents throughout the East.

British Library, India Office Library and Records, A/1/58

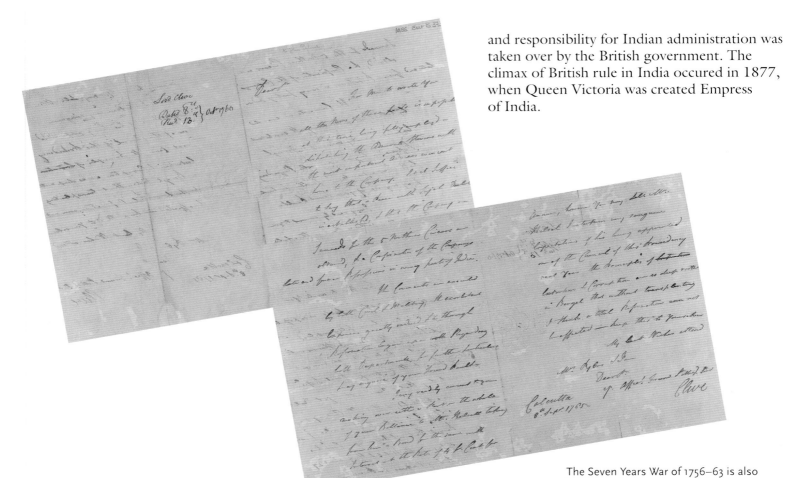

and responsibility for Indian administration was taken over by the British government. The climax of British rule in India occured in 1877, when Queen Victoria was created Empress of India.

The Seven Years War of 1756–63 is also known as the French and Indian war. It saw the pursuit of European conflicts not only in Europe but also in America and Asia. In India, the Nawab of Bengal sided with the French and sacked the East India Company settlement at Calcutta. Against the odds, a small force led by Robert Clive defeated the Nawab at Plassey. Clive replaced the Nawab with a pro-British ruler which paved the way for a huge expansion of British power in India. Clive was appointed governor and commander-in-chief in India in 1763, and in 1765 the Mughal emperor granted the East India Company responsibility for running the civil administration in Bengal, including the right to collect revenue. This is Clive's letter conveying news of this momentous grant.

British Library, India Office Library and Records, MSS Eur.B.373

This painting of Clive receiving the grant of the *diwani* of Bengal, Bihar and Orissa from the Mughal Emperor was commissioned by the East India Company from Benjamin West in the early 19th century.

British Library, India Office Library and Records, F.29

A Passage to India

Warren Hastings was the first British governor-general in India. He reformed the British administration and courts, in particular reorganising the export of opium to China. He fought a war against the powerful warriors known as the Mahrattas in western and central India. The letters he wrote while besieged at Chunar Fort in September 1781 after the revolt of Raja Chuit Singh at Benares are inscribed on slips of paper so small that they could be rolled up and put in quills to be smuggled through enemy lines. Hastings' career was controversial and in 1788 he was impeached. The trial lasted for seven years. Hastings was eventually acquitted, but he was a ruined man.

British Library, India Office Library and Records, MSS Eur.B.225

In 1883–4, Mrs Louisa Edwards, daughter of the Vicar of Rochdale and widow of the Perpetual Curate of Todmorden, visited her two sons, Lionel Edwards and Guilford Lindsay Edwards, who were engineers engaged in railway construction in different parts of India. Mrs Edwards kept a detailed journal of her tour, illustrated with charming watercolour drawings. Shown here is her drawing of her son Guilford's house at Gauri Bazar, Gorakhpur.

British Library, Additional MS. 43810, ff. 34v–35

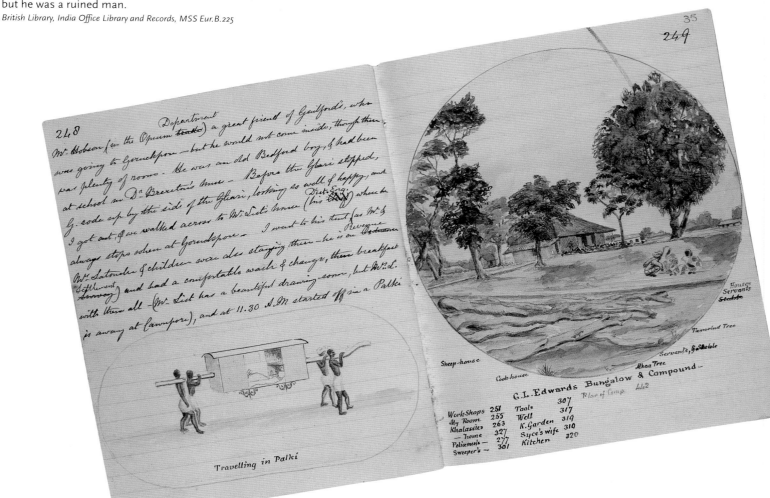

The term Methodism was used in the 17th century for a highly structured devotional regime, but during the 18th century came to be associated with the followers of the religious reformer John Wesley (1703–91), who is shown here. As students at Oxford, Wesley and his brother Charles had been members of a religious club devoted to biblical study and social work. Influenced by his Oxford friend George Whitefield, Wesley became a travelling preacher, addressing huge crowds in the open air all over Britain – his idea of a holiday in his 80th year was a preaching trip to Holland. Wesley encouraged the formation of Methodist societies, which held annual conferences, and developed a network of lay preachers. Although he insisted that he wanted to revitalise the Church of England, his activities were difficult to accommodate within the strict episcopal hierarchy of the established Church. After his death, his followers finally seceded from the Church of England, but this simply led to further disputes and divisions. It was only in the 1850s that these disputes began to be settled and the organisation of the Methodist Church placed on a firmer footing. By this time, the nonconformist churches were more influential in the new industrial districts than the Church of England. Methodism was criticised, however, for encouraging the poor passively to accept their lot.

In Wales, there was a parallel movement of religious revival which maintained close links with Wesley and Whitefield but was largely indigenous. On Whit Sunday 1735, Howel Harris experienced a religious conversion at Talgarth in Breconshire, and began preaching around the villages near Llangorse Lake. In 1737, he met Daniel Rowland, who had been preaching in the Aeron valley. Harris and Rowland concentrated on one stark theme: the hellfire that would await those who spurned Christ. Unlike Wesley or Whitefield, the Welsh reformers were strongly Calvinist in outlook. In the 1750s, Harris became obsessed with his scheme of establishing a religious 'family' at Trefeca, and was disowned by the Methodists, but the publication of the volume of hymns *Caniadau y rhai sydd ar y Môr o Wydr* (The Songs of Those Who Are on the Sea of Glass) by the great Welsh hymn writer William Williams of Pantycelyn prompted a 'second revival' and the settling of these differences. The second half of the eighteenth century saw a massive spread of nonconformity, particularly in north Wales. Although the Methodist revival was criticised by some for destroying traditional Welsh culture, it played a critical part in helping to preserve the Welsh language and developing a distinctive modern Welsh intellectual culture.

John Wesley at the age of 87
British Library, Additional MS. 41295, f. 21

The most distinctive power of the bishops of the Church of England was their authority to ordain priests. By the 1780s, Wesley was finding the necessity of seeking approval from a bishop to ordain his followers increasingly irksome. At Bristol, on 2 September 1784, Wesley ordained Richard Whatcoat and Thomas Vasey as elders for a mission to America. This is Wesley's draft of their certificates of appointment.
British Library, Additional MS. 41295, f. 20

This is the autograph manuscript of a hymn by William Williams (1717–91), the Welsh poet whose work played a crucial role in the spread of nonconformity in Wales. Williams was inspired to become a cleric by hearing Howel Harris at Talgarth. Refused ordination, he became an assistant to Daniel Rowland, and travelled the length and breadth of Wales preaching, selling copies of his hymns and – so it is said – vending tea. His most famous hymn, 'Guide Me O Thou Great Jehovah', became internationally known after it was published in a free English translation from the Welsh in 1772. The photograph shows his home at Pantycelyn farmhouse near Llandovery, Carmarthenshire.
National Library of Wales, NLW MS. 78A, f. 47r

The Industrial Revolution

etween 1750 and 1850, the face of Britain
changed. New manufacturing technologies
were developed and new energy sources
harnessed, encouraging the evolution of
factories on a large scale, and the rapid growth
of new industrial districts in the Glasgow area,
south Wales, and the industrial North and
Midlands of England. The industrial work force
increased apace, as agricultural labourers
decided that the harsh working and living
conditions of the new towns were a worthwhile
price to pay for a regular wage. The Industrial
Revolution made Britain by far the richest and
most opulent country in the world, but also
created a new type of society which, to many
commentators, seemed to offer a horrifying
vision of the future.

The modern term patent, used to register and protect rights
in new inventions, derives from the medieval letter patent –
monopolies in new inventions were at first granted by the
issue of a royal letter patent. This is the patent of invention
of Richard Arkwright's spinning frame of 1769. The machine
produced very strong cotton thread, so that for the first time
pure cotton cloth could be made. The spinning frame was
operated first by horses and mules, and later by water or
steam power, and spinning rapidly became a factory
enterprise rather than a home industry. Arkwright's own
factory at Cromford in Derbyshire was founded in 1771 and,
by 1782, was employing 5,000 people.
Public Record Office, C 73/13/9 nos. 30–33

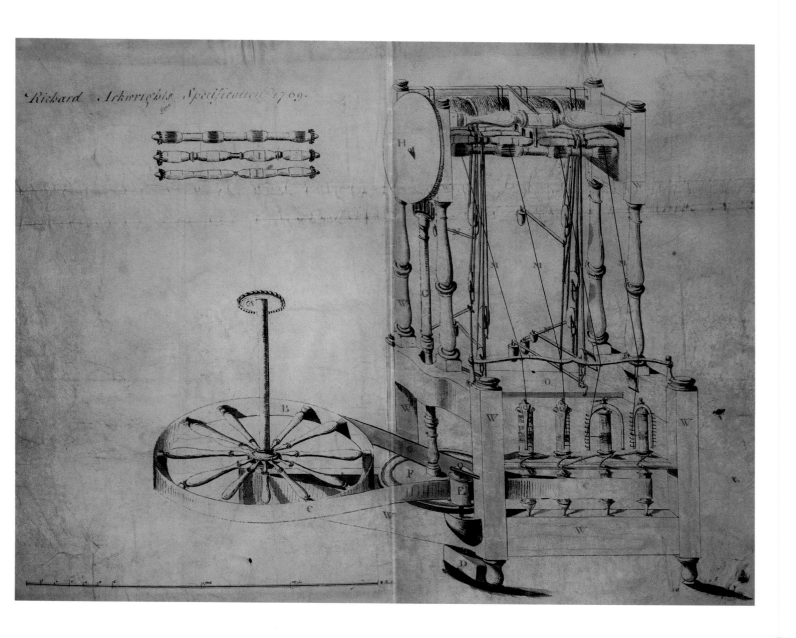

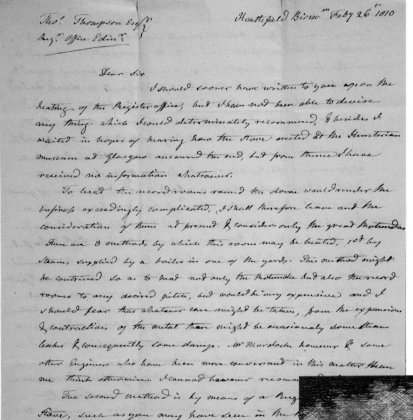

James Watt's improvements to Newcomen's steam engine provided the power behind the Industrial Revolution. Engineer, canal builder and instrument maker, Watt was called in to give his expert advice on the heating of Register House in Edinburgh, the home of the National Archives of Scotland. He found the problem a difficult one, and in this letter dated 26 February 1810 apologises for not writing earlier, 'but I have not been able to devise any thing which I could determinately recommend'.

National Archives of Scotland, SRO4/89/2

Ernest Jones was one of the leaders of the Chartist movement, which sought to achieve universal suffrage and the implementation of a radical programme of social reform in the middle of the 19th century. Jones was imprisoned from 1848 to 1850 for making seditious speeches, and this drawing was made by him while he was in prison, using paper and ink saved from his allowance for writing letters home. The view is imaginary, but shows Jones's abhorrence of the cramped, gloomy industrial town, where factories, churches, barracks and a new prison seem to press down on the populace. One of the Chartist aims was to regain the countryside for the people and to create smallholdings for townspeople.

British Library, Additional MS. 61979A, f. 29

The Industrial Revolution

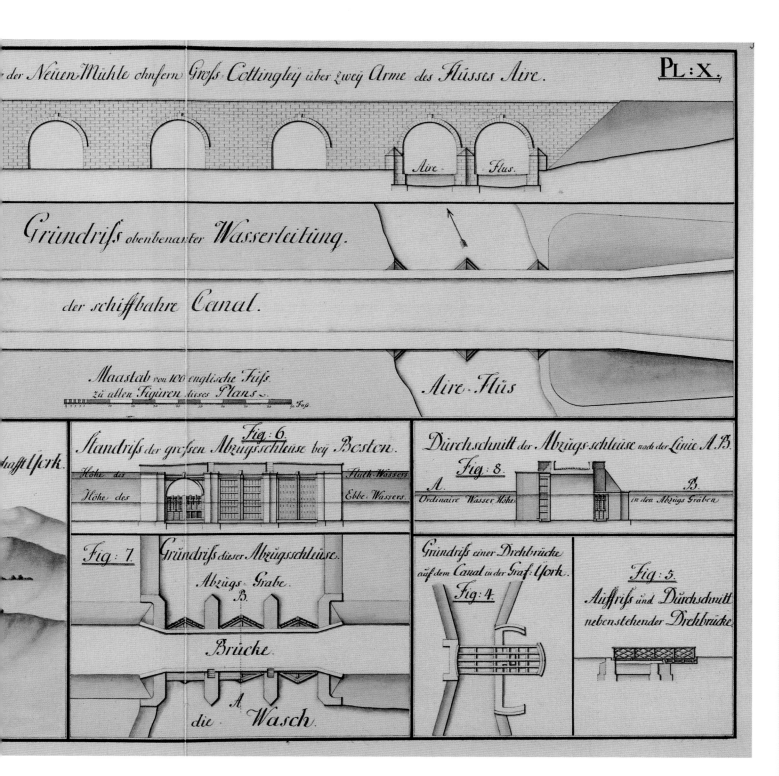

PL: X.

...der Neüen Mühle ohnfern Groß-Cottingley über zwey Arme des Flusses Aire.

Aire. Flus.

Grundriß obenbenanter Wasserleitung.

der schiffbahre Canal.

Maasstab von 100 englische Fuß, zu allen Figuren dieses Plans.

90 Fuß.

Aire. Flus

Fig: 6.
Standriß der großen Abzugsschleüse bey Boston.

Höhe des ... Fluth-Wassers.
Höhe des ... Ebbe. Wassers.

Durchschnitt der Abzugs-schleüse nach der Linie A.B.

Fig: 8.

A. ... B.

Ordinaire Wasser Höhe ... in den Abzugs Gräben.

Fig: 7. Grundriß dieser Abzugsschleüse.

Abzügs-Grabe.
B.

Brücke.

A.
die Wasch.

Grundriß einer Drehbrücke auf dem Canal in der Graf: York.

Fig: 4.

Fig: 5.
Auffriß und Durchschnitt nebenstehender Drehbrücke.

As the factory system grew, efficient transport systems were needed to supply factories with coal and raw materials and to allow the dispatch of manufactured goods. At first, these needs were met by the canal system, which grew rapidly in the second half of the 18th century. The locks, viaducts and tunnels of the new canals were masterpieces of enginnering. In 1777, the German engineer Johann Ludwig Hogrewe made a tour of English canals and prepared this beautifully illustrated report, which he presented to George III. The expertise developed in building the canal network was afterwards vital in the development of the railways, which by about 1840 had superseded the canals.

British Library, King's MS. 46, f. 58

The many changes which took place in British agriculture during the 18th and early 19th centuries have been designated, by analogy with the Industrial Revolution which took place at the same time, the 'Agricultural Revolution'. However, some of these changes were continuations of processes which had begun in the 17th century, and the relationship of the new agricultural techniques to the process of industrialisation is not clear. Moreover, agriculture continued to change and develop in the later 19th century, after the period of the supposed Agricultural Revolution.

The invention in 1714 by Jethro Tull of a horse-drawn hoe ushered in a period of enthusiasm for new agricultural techniques and a more scientific approach to farming. One of the most influential of the new agricultural writers was Arthur Young (1741–1820), who made his reputation with his 1768 survey of farming practice, *Six Weeks Tour through the Southern Counties of England and Wales*. He pioneered the use of statistical data in improving agriculture and also carried out the first detailed survey of the French rural economy. In 1794, he was appointed secretary to the new Board of Agriculture. Young's *magnum opus* was the compendious *Elements and Practice of Agriculture*, which was never published. These illustrations from the manuscript of Young's great work show the use of a Flemish scythe and an 'Earth Scuffer' invented by Ducket, a farmer greatly admired by Young.

British Library, Additional MS .34856, ff. 270, 278

The Agricultural Revolution

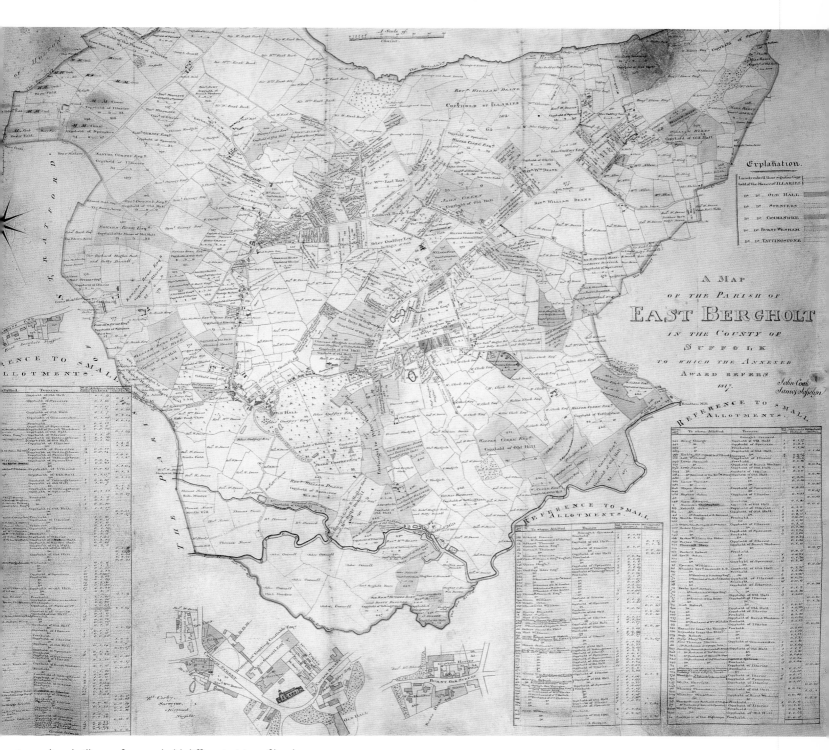

In medieval villages, farmers held different strips of land distributed in three or four open fields surrounding the village. Grazing and other rights were controlled communally. From the 17th century, the process of enclosure, whereby these strips were consolidated to form separate holdings of the modern type, gained momentum. Smaller farmers suffered greatly as a result of enclosures, since communal rights were lost. Nearly 6 million acres of land was enclosed between 1750 and 1815. When enclosure took place, maps showing the distribution of land holdings were drawn up. This enclosure map of 1817 is for East Bergholt in Suffolk, and includes the site of Flatford Mill, made famous by John Constable's painting.

Public Record Office, MR 247

The American War of Independence is an event from which Britain has perhaps still not recovered, remaining uncertain in its relationship with its former colony which has become the world's most powerful state. The Stamp Act of 1763 imposed duty on all official papers, newspapers, pamphlets, playing cards and dice, and was intended to recoup some of the costs of defending America during the Seven Years War. This measure encountered fierce resistance in America. Although it was repealed, the British government insisted on its right to impose taxes in America. In 1770, all taxes were repealed except that on tea, which the British Prime Minister insisted was his 'peppercorn of principle', the emblem of the British government's right to impose taxes in America. Continuing protests against the tea duty culminated in the famous destruction of tea cargoes at the Boston Tea Party of 1773. The British tried to undermine the solidarity of the American colonies, but in 1774 they affirmed their unity at the first continental congress. In 1775, the colonies were declared

This letter of Samuel Cooper of Boston to Benjamin Franklin, the American founding father and scientist, is dated 17 December 1783, and describes the Boston Tea Party, which had taken place the previous day. He describes how 'two or three hundred Persons in Dress & appearance like Indians, passed by the old South Meeting House, where the Assembly was held, gave a War Hoop, & hasten'd to the Wharf where all the Tea Ships lay, and demanding the Tea, which was given up to them without the least Resistance, they soon emptied all the Chests into the Harbor'. This letter is preserved in the library of the British king at the time, George III.
British Library, King's MS. 203, f. 16

(opposite left) A map showing Boston, the leading town of Massachusetts Bay Province and the centre of American resistance to the British. Boston was at this time the most important port in America, the heart of a commercial empire extending from North Carolina to Nova Scotia. With a population of 250,000 and a full treasury, Massachusetts Bay Province became the most vociferous and militant opponent of British rule in America.
Public Record Office, CO 700/Mass/14

(opposite top right) British attempts to make an example of Massachusetts by the enactment of the 'Intolerable Acts' caused the first congress of representatives of all thirteen colonies to be convened. The congress resolved to support Massachusetts by boycotting all British goods, but also sent this petition to George III asking for a return to the system of colonial administration which had prevailed until 1763 and an end to the attempts to impose taxes from London: 'From this destructive system of colony administration adopted since the conclusion of the last war, have flowed those distresses dangers fears and jealousies that overwhelm your majesty's dutiful colonists with affliction...We ask but for peace, liberty and safety'.
Public Record Office, CO 5/75 pt. 2, f. 239

(opposite bottom right) View of the Battle of Bunker Hill and the burning of Charlestown on 17 June 1775. Bunker Hill was one of the first major engagements of the war. More than 18,000 American troops surrounding Boston were driven back by British forces supported by naval gunfire, with great losses on both sides, while the settlement of Charlestown was destroyed by shells fired from Boston.
British Library, Cup. 1247.cc.17

The American Declaration of Independence, one of the most famous texts in the world, was drafted by Thomas Jefferson and others. It was approved by Congress on 4 July 1776 and printed that very night by John Dunlop of Philadelphia. Only 22 copies of Dunlop's first printing of the Declaration of Independence are known to have survived. This one, now preserved in the Public Record Office, was enclosed in a letter sent to the Admiralty.

Public Record Office, ADM 1/487, f. 28

Following the defeat at Yorktown, the House of Commons passed a resolution declaring that anyone who urged the continuation of the war in America should be considered an enemy of the king and country. The Prime Minister, Lord North, resigned, and George III declared that 'the fatal day is come'. Articles of peace recognising the United States as an independent power were signed in November 1782; a formal treaty for the cessation of hostilities between the United States and Britain was eventually ratified on 15 April 1783. This is a proclamation announcing the ratification of the treaty.

Public Record Office, CO 5/109, f. 106

to be rebellious, and the first clashes between British and American troops took place. A year later, the Americans had driven the British out of Boston and the Declaration of Independence had been signed. Following a devastating defeat at Saratoga in October 1777, the British offered to repeal all offensive legislation and recognise congress, but French offers of help encouraged the Americans to fight on and in June 1778 the French joined the war, followed by the Spanish in 1779. Britain was threatened with invasion by France and Spain, attempts by Ireland to secure independence, and war in southern India. The

No Taxation Without Representation

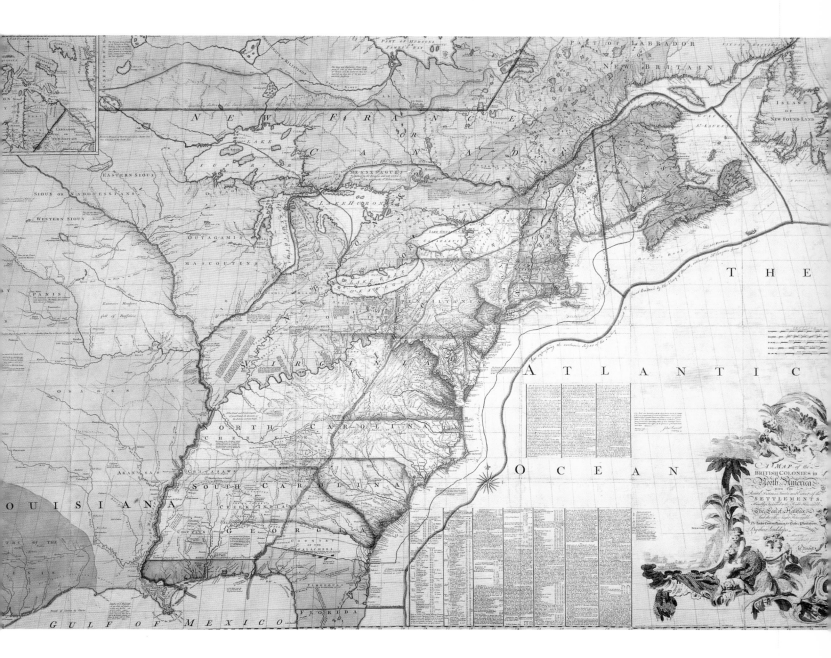

campaign in America moved to the south, where at first the British scored some successes, but, following the defeat of the British fleet at the battle of Chesapeake and the surrender of the English commander Lord Cornwallis at Yorktown, the British government decided to stop trying to use force against the American colonies, and signed the Peace of Versailles recognising American independence in September 1783.

This map is the one on which the British negotiators for peace with the Americans marked out their interpretation of the boundary between the United States and the provinces which later formed Canada. The new border was marked in red, so the map became known as the 'Red-lined map'. It was presented to George III to show him how the settlement worked on the ground. As the map was not included in the final treaty and as the printed map itself contained inaccuracies, further arbitration was later required.

British Library, K. 118.d.26 (K. Top. cxviii.49.b)

James Cook (1728–79) learned his craft as a seaman in the east coast coal trade. Although he had almost attained the rank of master as a merchant seaman, in 1755 he moved across to the navy as an able seaman, a lower level. His skills as a navigator were quickly noticed, and in 1759 he successfully piloted the *Pembroke* through the hazardous waters of the St Lawrence River, thus facilitating Wolfe's successful attack on Quebec. In 1767 Cook, by now a lieutenant, was appointed to command the *Endeavour* on a voyage to Tahiti to make astronomical observations for the Royal Society. On this first Pacific voyage, which lasted from 1768–70, Cook also successfully explored and mapped New Zealand, the eastern coast of Australia, and Hawaii. During his second Pacific voyage from 1772–5, he crossed the Antarctic circle, penetrating to within 1300 miles of the South Pole and mapping part of the coast of Antarctica. During his third voyage, in which he explored the north-west coast of America, Cook was killed during a skirmish with natives in Hawaii.

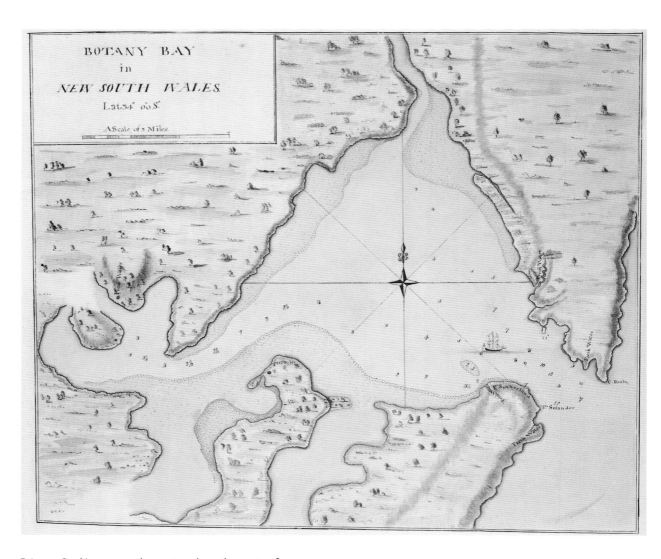

Prior to Cook's voyage, the west and south coasts of Australia had been visited by other European explorers, but the east coast was unexplored. Cook first sighted the eastern coast of Australia on 19 April 1770, and landed at Botany Bay, so called because of the large number of previously unknown plants collected there by the expedition's scientists. This is the chart made of Botany Bay during Cook's stay there, drawn probably by Cook himself.
British Library, Additional MS. 31360, f. 32

Captain Cook and Australia

After leaving Botany Bay, Cook's ship ran aground on the Great Barrier Reef, and he was forced to stop in the Endeavour River to effect repairs. While the *Endeavour* was under repair, the expedition artist, Sydney Parkinson, drew this view, which is the first known depiction of Australia's landscape.

British Library, Additional MS. 23920, f. 36

Transportation was introduced as an alternative to the death penalty in the 17th century. America was the initially favoured destination for transported convicts; by 1776, about a thousand a year were being sent there. With the loss of the American colonies, there was nowhere for new convicts to be sent, and the government was forced to resort to the expedient of keeping prisoners on old ships in the Thames. Cook's discoveries in Australia offered a solution to this problem, and on 13 May 1787 an eleven-strong fleet of Royal Navy ships under the command of Captain Arthur Phillip bearing more than a thousand people sailed from Portsmouth, headed for New South Wales. This is the register of convicts who were carried on that first fleet. The extremely dangerous voyage was accomplished in about 250 days with the loss of only 32 convicts. Captain Phillip became the first governor of the new colony. Finding Botany Bay unsuitable for habitation, he moved north to Sydney Cove, and on 26 January 1788 officially founded the new settlement.

Public Record Office, HO 10/7, ff. 32v–33

Much of the wealth of 18th-century Britain was built on the slave trade. Used for work on sugar and tobacco plantations in Brazil, the Caribbean and in the southern colonies of mainland North America, over six million slaves were imported into North and South America during the 18th century. Many of them were obtained in Africa by the exchange of manufactured and luxury goods, then carried across the Atlantic in horrific conditions, packed into the holds of ships. In the late 18th century, British public opinion increasingly turned against the slave trade, and the Somerset case in 1772 abolished slavery on English and Welsh soil. This prompted a major public campaign in 1787–8 against the slave trade, resulting in 1807 in the outlawing of slave transportation on British ships and of their import into British colonies. A leading figure in this movement was the campaigning evangelical philanthropist William Wilberforce (1759–1833). In the year of Wilberforce's death, all slaves in British dominions were finally emancipated.

In 1785, the tiny Liverpool ship, *Mangovo George*, took a cargo of about 1800 items, such as cotton, guns, swords and brandy, to the west coast of Africa, then sailed down the coast, exchanging these goods for slaves. The first entry reads 'Bought of the Duke of Cumberland [a nickname for the man from whom the slaves were purchased] one boy 3/11 [the boy's height, that is three foot eleven inches]'. The goods exchanged for the boy are then listed. They include fabric, a gun, gunpowder, a cutlass, a spoon and a razor.
British Library, Additional MS. 43841, f. 8

The Slave Trade

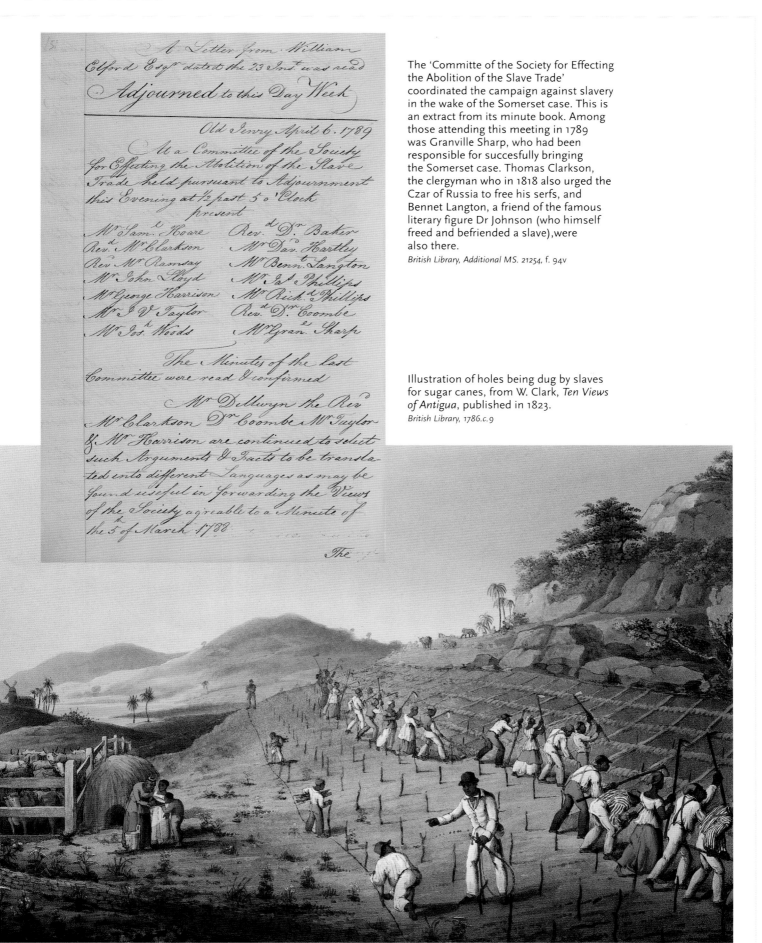

The 'Committe of the Society for Effecting the Abolition of the Slave Trade' coordinated the campaign against slavery in the wake of the Somerset case. This is an extract from its minute book. Among those attending this meeting in 1789 was Granville Sharp, who had been responsible for succesfully bringing the Somerset case. Thomas Clarkson, the clergyman who in 1818 also urged the Czar of Russia to free his serfs, and Bennet Langton, a friend of the famous literary figure Dr Johnson (who himself freed and befriended a slave),were also there.
British Library, Additional MS. 21254, f. 94v

Illustration of holes being dug by slaves for sugar canes, from W. Clark, *Ten Views of Antigua*, published in 1823.
British Library, 1786.c.9

The war against France which was a reaction to the French Revolution and lasted from 1793 to 1815, with a break from 1802–3, seems in many ways to encapsulate many of the British national myths – the importance of seapower, the invincibility of an island against conquest, Britain standing alone against a tyrant. However, the motives for the war were less glorious, and it was as much due to British government concern that the revolution might spread to Britain as alarm at French territorial annexations. Although the first period of the war was marked by Nelson's victories at the Nile and Copenhagen, it also saw a mutiny of the fleet at Spithead and a rising supported by the French in Ireland. The rise of Napoleon and his seizure of further territory in Europe led to a renewal of war and Napoleon assembled an invasion force at Boulogne. Nelson's victory at Trafalgar secured British control of the Channel and saw off the threat of invasion. However, by 1806 Napoleon had defeated Britain's

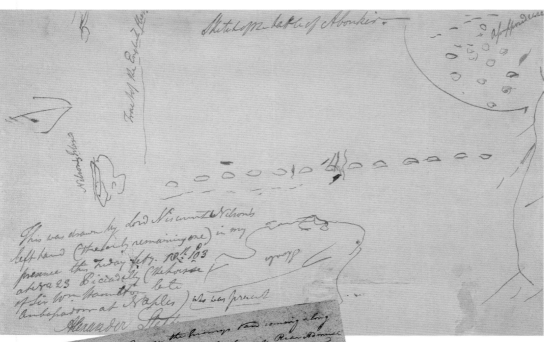

Horatio Nelson, 1st Viscount Nelson (1758–1805), the great English naval commander, lost his right arm during an attack on Santa Cruz in Tenerife in 1797. He was forced to learn to use his left hand for writing. This plan illustrating his great victory at the Battle of the Nile in 1798, in which the French Mediterranean fleet was devastated, stranding French forces in Egypt and ensuring British naval superiority in the Mediterranean, was drawn by Nelson with his left hand in 1803.
British Library, Additional MS. 18676

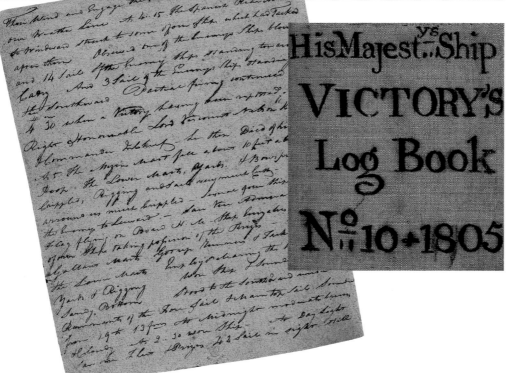

The log-book of Nelson's flagship, the *Victory*, was kept by Thomas Atkinson, the sailing-master of the ship. The original log-book, carefully wrapped in sail-cloth, remained in Atkinson's possession; a fair copy was made which was sent to the Admiralty. Shown here is the sail-cloth cover of Atkinson's book, and the page describing Nelson's death during the Battle of Trafalgar. The description of Nelson's death reads: 'Partial firing continued until 4^h 30^m a Victory having been reported to the Rt Honourable Lord Viscount Nelson KB Commander in Chief he then died of his Wounds'.
British Library, Additional MS. 39862, f. 35v

England Expects

continental allies, and Britain stood alone. Like Hitler in the following century, Napoleon's achilles heel was Russia. By 1812, Franco-Russian relations had deteriorated so badly that Napoleon decided to conquer Russia, but he failed to defeat the Russians, and was forced to fall back across Europe. Prussia and Austria took the opportunity to throw off the Napoleonic yoke. At the same time, the Spanish, supported by British forces commanded by the Duke of Wellington, had risen up against Napoleon's brother, who had been sent to rule them, and gradually forced the French out. In 1814, the allies entered Paris. Napoleon was exiled to Elba, but in 1815 he escaped, and quickly raised an army of Frenchmen who hated the allied domination of their country. However, Napoleon was defeated near Waterloo, a town south of Brussels. Napoleon was sent to the remote Atlantic island of St Helena under British custody, where he remained until 1821, when he died of arsenic poisoning, caused by the damp wallpaper in his villa.

Although these memorable incidents are what is popularly known of these wars, in many ways it was the administrative innovations forced by the war, such as the introduction of income tax, censuses, government intervention in agriculture, and the mobilisation of large numbers of civilians, which were to be of greater long-term importance in the development of a modern British state.

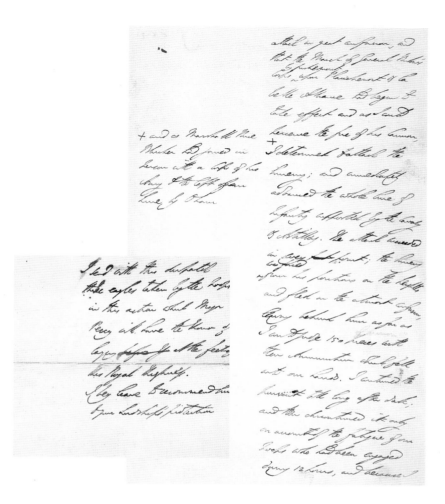

This is the Duke of Wellington's draft of his dispatch to Lord Bathurst, the Principal Secretary of State for the War Department, reporting his victory over Napoleon at Waterloo. It is dated 'Waterloo, June 19th. 1815', the day after the battle. The two pages shown record the moment at which the outcome of the battle became clear and, as a postscript to the main text, the sending of captured standards to be laid at the feet of the Prince Regent. A fair copy made from this draft was signed by the Duke at Brussels and taken to London by Major the Hon. Henry Percy, who arrived with it late on the evening of 21 June.
British Library, Additional MS. 69850

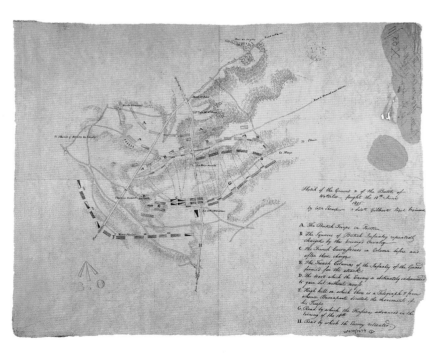

Map of the Battle of Waterloo, 18 June 1815. Napoleon spent almost a whole day unsuccessfully trying to dislodge the British from their position on a ridge south of the town. The eventual arrival of the Prussians enabled the allies to launch a counterattack against the French and sweep them back towards Paris.
Public Record Office, MPW 387 (1)

The period immediately after the French Revolution was one of intense intellectual ferment throughout Europe, and in Britain a remarkable generation of writers challenged old artistic conventions, pioneered new forms and played an important part in shaping national self-perceptions. In Scotland, Sir Walter Scott and Robert Burns played critical roles in defining modern Scottish culture. In England, the period from 1790 to 1820 saw an extraordinary array of great writers at work, including Samuel Taylor Coleridge, John Keats, Lord Byron and Percy Bysshe Shelley. Jane Austen helped establish the novel as the most characteristic English literary form and painted a picture of English society which is still influential today. William Wordsworth encouraged contemporaries to look at the English landscape with new eyes, while William Blake developed a unique mystical vision of England.

Walter Scott was already the most famous poet in Europe when he suddenly emerged as the author of prose fiction with the (anonymous) publication of *Waverley* in 1814. Part of Scott's manuscript is shown here. *Waverley* was the first historical novel, and it caused a sensation. It deals with themes that fascinated Scott's contemporaries, and which continue to fascinate today: the lost cause of Jacobitism and the romance of the '45 rebellion, and the depiction of societies (both Highland and Lowland) in the course of profound change. The book did much to make Scotland a popular theme in life, art, travel and fashion in the early 19th century, an enthusiasm which reached its peak in the Victorian period.
National Library of Scotland, Adv.MS.1.1.0

After the publication of the Kilmarnock edition of his poems in July 1786, Robert Burns visited Edinburgh, where he was feted by fashionable society. Among the people Burns met in this social whirl was Mrs Agnes McLehose with whom he established a platonic relationship. Their correspondence, in which they used the arcadian pseudonyms of 'Sylvander' and 'Clarinda', is one of the most famous examples of stylised romantic letter writing. After their final meeting on 6 December 1791, which occurred shortly before Mrs McLehose left for Jamaica for a hoped-for reconciliation with her estranged husband, 'Clarinda' received a letter from Burns in which he expressed his feelings in verse: Ae fond kiss, & then we sever;/Ae fareweel, & then for ever!...Had we never lov'd sae kindly/Had we never lov'd sae blindly'.
National Library of Scotland, MS 586, no. 1134, f. 32

A Romantic View

Jane Austen's will (right) was written by her on 27 April 1817 at Winchester, where she died and was buried in the cathedral. The executrix and chief beneficiary of the will was Jane's sister Cassandra, who had nursed her through her last illness. The total estate came to less than £800.
Public Record Office, PROB 1/78

To the Printer

after the Poem (in the set under the title of "Moods of my own mind") beginning "The Cock is crowing" please to insert the two following properly numbered & number the succeeding &c. accordingly

I wandered lonely as a Cloud
That floats on high o'er Vales and Hills,
When all at once I saw a crowd
A host of dancing Daffodils;
Along the Lake beneath the trees
Ten thousand dancing in the breeze.

The Waves beside them danced, but they
Outdid the sparkling Waves in glee:—
A Poet could not but be gay
In such a laughing company:
I gaz'd – and gaz'd – but little thought
What wealth the shew to me had brought.

For oft when on my couch I lie
In vacant, or in pensive mood,
They flash upon that inward eye
Which is the bliss of solitude
And then my heart with pleasure fills,
And dances with the Daffodils.

Who fancied what a pretty sight
This Rock would be if edged around
With living Snowdrops? circlet bright!

(above) The Romantic poets worshipped the outdoors, and first drew attention to the beauties of such landscapes as great lakes, mountains and sweeping bays. The most influential English nature poet of this period was William Wordsworth. This is an autograph copy of one of his most famous nature lyrics, *To Daffodils*, which appeared in *Poems, in Two Volumes* in 1807.
British Library, Additional MS. 47864, f. 80

(right) *Milton* was the last of William Blake's illuminated books, which combined poems and pictures in a unique fashion. The preface calls on the 'young men of the New Age' to restore true art to its proper rank and renounce war. It concludes with a poem denouncing the 'dark Satanic Mills' of contemporary materialism, and calls for the building of Jerusalem, the city of art, in 'England's green & pleasant land'. This poem has become a well-known patriotic song in its setting by Sir Charles Hubert Parry, written in 1916. Of the four surviving copies of *Milton*, only two contain the preface with the famous lyric.
British Museum, Department of Prints and Drawings

PREFACE.

Between 1793 and 1815 the British government alienated increasingly large sections of the population by its massive expenditure – £1,500 million, scraped together from loans and heavy taxation – on the Napoleonic wars and its repressive measures to control dissent. The radical writer William Cobbett considered that the war had further strengthened the grip on society of what he called 'The Thing', the stranglehold of the rich on the poor, and Shelley, a literary radical, urged:

> 'Men of England, wherefore plough
> For the Lords who lay ye low?'

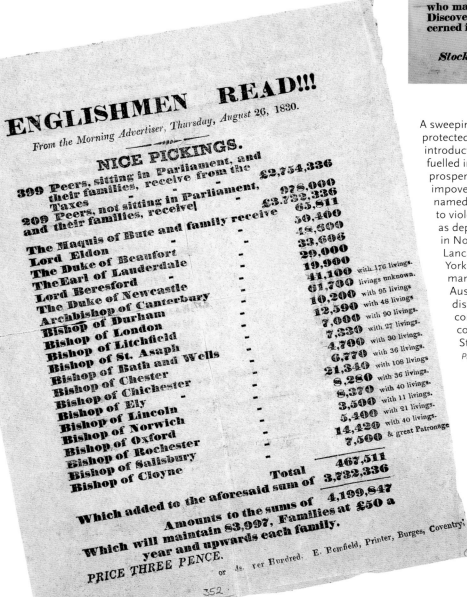

A sweeping away of the old regulations which had protected trade practices in textiles encouraged the introduction of new machines of mass production, and fuelled industrialisation and, for some, economic prosperity. Between 1811 and 1816, powerless and impoverished groups of textile workers, the Luddites, named after their mythical leader Captain Ludd, turned to violence against the hated machines which they saw as depriving them of their livelihoods. Having begun in Nottinghamshire, the unrest spread across Lancashire, Cheshire, Derbyshire, Leicestershire and Yorkshire, but was put down with great severity: many Luddites were hanged or transported to Australia as convicts. The gravity with which the disturbances were viewed is shown by this poster condemning Luddite attack on the warehouse of a cotton manufacturer, Mr William Radcliffe, of Stockport, Cheshire, 1812.

Public Record Office, HO 1/1/1 pt 1, f. 8

This seditious pamphlet attacking the House of Lords, from 1830, gives a flavour of the continuing strength of radical opinion during the following decade.

Public Record Office, HO 44/22, no. 352

Radicalism and Reform

(left) Riots and strikes continued in 1817 and 1818, and finally in Manchester on 16 August 1819 the local magistrates ordered the yeomanry to break up a huge but peaceful demonstration at St Peter's fields. Eleven were killed in this, the Peterloo Massacre, which was effective in quelling immediate dissent but, as this hostile lithograph demonstrates, sharpened opposition to the repressive government in the longer term.

Public Record Office, HO 42/199/MPI 134

(above) In Wales there were major although unsuccessful upheavals in 1842–44, partly a reaction to the imposition of toll charges on public roads. They were known as the Rebecca Riots because groups of rioters attacked the toll houses dressed up as women and took on the identity of Rebecca and her daughters, following the prophecy in Genesis that 'the seed of Rebecca would possess the gate of those which hate them'. This contemporary lithograph shows Rebecca on horseback wielding an axe at a toll-gate.

National Library of Wales

(above) Although the 1820s saw some liberalisation with, for example, the repeal of antitrade union legislation and, in 1829, Catholic Emancipation, parliamentary reform still remained the prize for working class radicals and middle class liberals alike. But such was the extent of opposition within the House of Lords itself that the first Reform Act of 1832, rejected twice by them, was finally passed by nine votes in the face of widespread and largescale civil disturbances across the land. The size of the electorate was increased to encompass about one-fifth of the male population, and there was a shift away from the Rotten Boroughs, allowing the new industrial areas such as Birmingham and Manchester to return MPs for the first time. This is the opening of the Reform Act, as formally enrolled in the Parliament Roll.

Public Record Office, C 65/3264

(right) The name of Rebecca remained a potent one in Wales. This call to arms in both Welsh and English was issued in Rebecca's name on 18 September 1854 against the levying of church rates by the Anglican Church in a country which was predominently nonconformist.

National Library of Wales

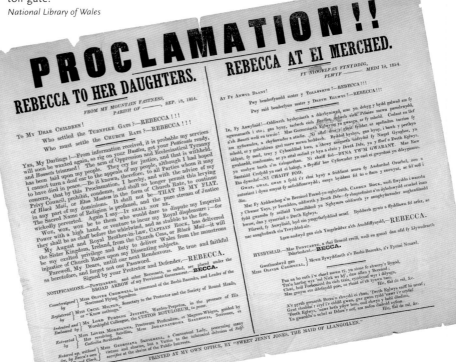

Although Captain Cook had claimed New Zealand for the British crown in 1769, no colony had been established there. In 1839, Edward Gibbon Wakefield, who had developed a number of influential theories about methods of colonisation during a spell in prison, founded the New Zealand Company to facilitate systematic immigration. Concerned about the activities of Wakefield's company and to forestall annexation of New Zealand by the French, the British government sent Captain William Hobson to treat with the Maori chiefs. Hobson negotiated the Treaty of Waitangi whereby the Maori accepted British rule in return for assurances about land rights. A week after Hobson's arrival, Wakefield's colonists appeared on board their ship the *Tory*, and proposed to take possession of substantial tracts of Maori land, which the New Zealand Company claimed to have bought and for which the colonists had been charged. Hobson refused to recognise the company's purchases, and a lengthy dispute ensued, which was not settled by the time Hobson died in 1842. These problems were eventually resolved by Sir George Grey, who sought to try and strike a balance between the demands of the colonists and the rights of the Maoris. A central government with an elected parliament and cabinet was established in 1856. However, disputes about land were to spark off a series of violent conflicts between the Maori and European settlers which persisted until 1872.

This portrait of a Maori was made by Sydney Parkinson during Cook's first visit to New Zealand in 1770.
British Library, Additional MS. 23920, f. 55

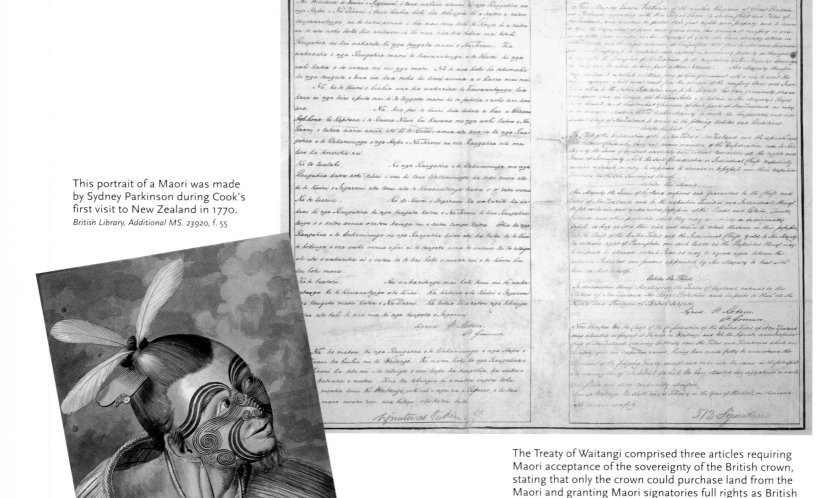

The Treaty of Waitangi comprised three articles requiring Maori acceptance of the sovereignty of the British crown, stating that only the crown could purchase land from the Maori and granting Maori signatories full rights as British subjects. The treaty was translated by missionaries and read on 5 February 1840 to a gathering of chiefs, who were divided as to whether the treaty would be a solemn contract protecting their interests or an instrument of enslavement. On 6 February 1840, 46 chiefs signed the treaty, a number that later swelled to 500.
Public Record Office, CO 209/7, f. 178

Contacts with the East

In 1793, George Macartney, 1st Viscount Macartney, travelled to Peking as ambassador of King George III, the first formal diplomatic contact between the two most powerful empires in the world at that time. Macartney hoped to open up Chinese markets to British merchants, and also sought to provide a flamboyant demonstration of the superiority of British science and culture. Macartney's mission became notorious for his refusal to 'kowtow' and perform the ritual obeisance which foreign visitors were expected to make before the Emperor. His embassy has therefore been seen as an expression of the way in which Europe was increasingly seeking to impose its values on the rest of the world. This view of a Chinese town was made during the mission by Sir John Barrow, comptroller of Macartney's household during the trip to China and afterwards Secretary to the Admiralty.

British Library, Additional MS. 33931, f. 14

Britain's involvement with Hong Kong illustrated the positive and negative aspects of the British Empire. Britain objected to Chinese attempts to stop the British selling opium to the local population and declared war on China. This was an uneven match, and China was quickly overwhelmed. By this document, the Treaty of Nanking of 1842, the Chinese were forced to concede to Britain Hong Kong Island in the Pearl River delta, as well as to pay compensation for the loss of the opium and to open up five named ports to British ships. In 1860, China was forced to expand Hong Kong by the grant of mainland Kowloon and in 1898 it gave Britain a 99-year lease on the New Territories. Despite the unpropitious origins of British rule in Hong Kong, the high quality of British administration and justice during the 20th century helped to make Hong Kong one of the richest cities in the world by the time it was returned to China in 1997.

Public Record Office, FO 93/23/1B

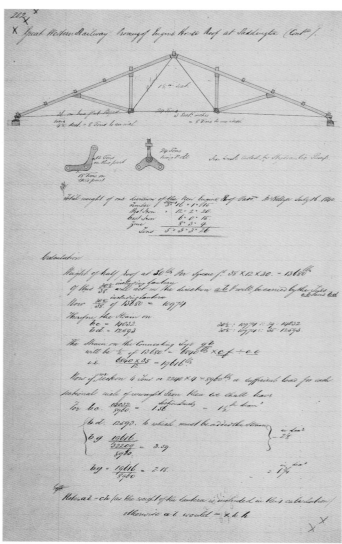

In 1800 the canals were Britain's industrial arteries and there was a mere 200 miles of railway tracks of different gauges, constructed some of wood, others of iron, and carrying horse-drawn wagons. Within 40 years the canals were eclipsed by the dramatic development of this new form of transport. But the early development of the railways was slow and faltering: in 1804 Richard Trevithick developed a steam traction engine, the *New Castle*, for a Welsh tramway, but it proved unreliable since its weight was too great for the rails, and other inventors – among them William Hedley with his *Puffing Billy* (1813) – experienced the same problems. Nevertheless by 1830 parliament had authorised the building of 375 miles of railway lines for public use, carrying passengers and freight, amongst them the pioneering Stockton and Darlington Railway, opened in 1825 by the highly talented George Stephenson, and the Liverpool and Manchester Railway, opened in 1829. In the same year trials were held to establish the most effective steam engine: the winner was *Rocket*, also designed by George Stephenson, which used a multiple fire-tube boiler rather than a single flue.

Public Record Office, COPY 1/31, f. 60

In 1834 Stephenson set the course of steam locomotion for a century with his production model of the *Rocket*, known as the *Patentee*; this and the development of stronger rolled iron rails enabled the railway boom to take off in Britain. By 1840 there were almost 2,400 miles of track, and by 1850, more than 8,000 miles, stretching from Plymouth to Aberdeen. A key figure in the development of the railways was the visionary entrepreneur Isambard Kingdom Brunel. His diverse engineering works – such as the Clifton Suspension Bridge in Bristol and the iron transatlantic steamers the *Great Western* and the *Great Britain* – were all on the grand scale. In 1833, Brunel was appointed engineer to the Great Western Railway, which was built using a broad seven-foot gauge to allow greater speed and stability. The London terminus for the Great Western was at Paddington; this is one of Brunel's drawings for the engine shed roof at Paddington.

Public Record Office, RAIL 1149/9, f. 97r.

The Railway Age

By 1870 Britain had almost 13,500 miles of railways, and train speeds were increasing: in 1895, two rival locomotives raced from London and Aberdeen at an average of more than 60 miles an hour. The railway infrastructure, too, was becoming increasingly sophisticated: the longest underwater rail tunnel in the world, the Severn Tunnel, running under the Bristol Channel, was opened in 1886, followed four years later by the Forth Railway Bridge (above), which was described as the eighth wonder of the modern world. 4600 men from all over Europe were employed at the height of its construction.

National Archives of Scotland, BR/FOR/4/34/291

Although the railways came later to London than to northern England – the London and Greenwich Railway was launched in 1836 – the world's first earliest underground railway, in the form of the Metropolitan Line, was opened in the capital in 1863. This was essentially a roofed-in trench, and other such lines were soon to follow. The District Line (first known as the Metropolitan District railway) started operation between South Kensington and Westminster in 1868. The line was then extended eastwards, the rails being laid within the new Thames Embankment. By 1887, when this timetable was published, the line had also been pushed westwards as far as Richmond and Ealing Broadway (there had even briefly been a service to Windsor). These early underground trains were pulled by steam engines which were specially adapted to turn used steam into water.

Public Record Office, COPY 1/80, f. 492

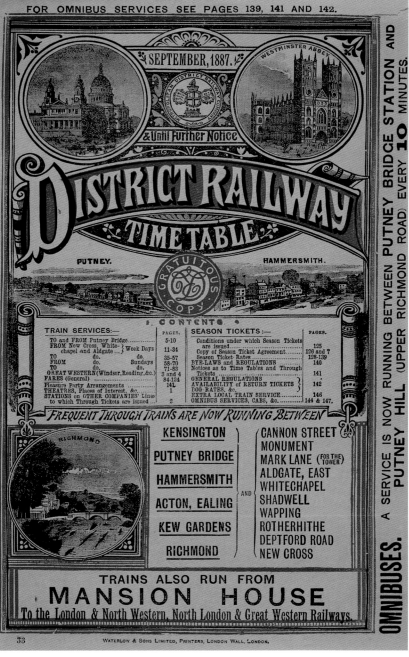

Queen Victoria (1819–1901) came to the throne in 1837 and is the longest-reigning monarch in British history. Although Victoria's name is now seen as synonymous with a period of unparalleled British power and prosperity, her status as a national matriarch was achieved only in the last years of her reign. In 1840, Victoria married her first cousin, Prince Albert of Saxe-Coburg-Gotha (1819–61). Victoria was devoted to Albert and they had nine children, but there was public suspicion of Albert because of his German origins and his determination to be a modernising and progressive force in British life. Albert's early death from typhoid threw Victoria into inconsolable grief, and she effectively retired from public life. Accusations of dereliction of duty and rumours about Victoria's relationship with her servant John Brown placed the future of the monarchy itself in doubt. Victoria was coaxed back into public life by Disraeli, and threw herself into her official duties with renewed vigour. By the time of the Golden and Diamond Jubilees of her accession in 1887 and 1897 respectively, not only was Victoria's popularity assured, but the monarchy had assumed its distinctive place in national life. The role of the monarch was by now almost entirely ceremonial, but was nevertheless vital in holding together Britain and its dominions, providing the most obvious personal link between not only the peoples of Britain itself but also the inhabitants of its far-flung Empire.

These photographs of Victoria and Albert are taken from the photograph album of one of Victoria's ladies-in-waiting, Jane, Lady Waterpark.
British Library, Additional MS. 60751, f. 1

The first censuses from 1801 onwards merely asked enumerators to establish overall figures for population in their areas. The first modern census was in 1841 when details were collected of such information as the name, age, sex, occupation and so on of each person. Enumerators' returns for censuses from 1841 are an incomparable source of genealogical and social information. This is the return for Buckingham Palace on census night, 6 June 1841.
Public Record Office, HO 107/740/35, f. 3v

Victoria and Albert

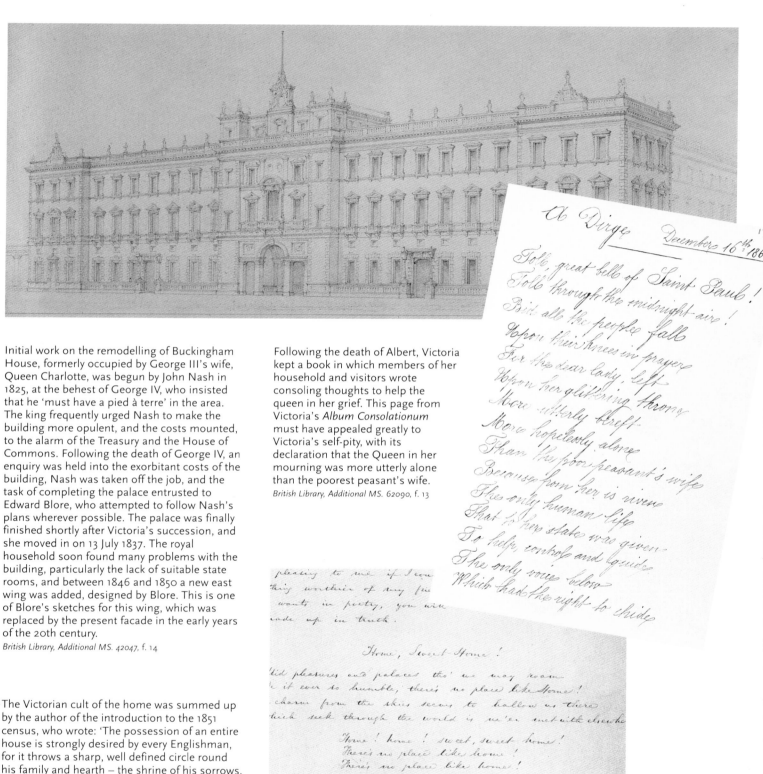

Initial work on the remodelling of Buckingham House, formerly occupied by George III's wife, Queen Charlotte, was begun by John Nash in 1825, at the behest of George IV, who insisted that he 'must have a pied à terre' in the area. The king frequently urged Nash to make the building more opulent, and the costs mounted, to the alarm of the Treasury and the House of Commons. Following the death of George IV, an enquiry was held into the exorbitant costs of the building, Nash was taken off the job, and the task of completing the palace entrusted to Edward Blore, who attempted to follow Nash's plans wherever possible. The palace was finally finished shortly after Victoria's succession, and she moved in on 13 July 1837. The royal household soon found many problems with the building, particularly the lack of suitable state rooms, and between 1846 and 1850 a new east wing was added, designed by Blore. This is one of Blore's sketches for this wing, which was replaced by the present facade in the early years of the 20th century.

British Library, Additional MS. 42047, f. 14

Following the death of Albert, Victoria kept a book in which members of her household and visitors wrote consoling thoughts to help the queen in her grief. This page from Victoria's *Album Consolationum* must have appealed greatly to Victoria's self-pity, with its declaration that the Queen in her mourning was more utterly alone than the poorest peasant's wife.

British Library, Additional MS. 62090, f. 13

The Victorian cult of the home was summed up by the author of the introduction to the 1851 census, who wrote: 'The possession of an entire house is strongly desired by every Englishman, for it throws a sharp, well defined circle round his family and hearth – the shrine of his sorrows, joys and meditations'. Victoria and Albert were the high priests of this domestic cult, providing a model of family life which the whole nation sought to emulate. The Victorian preoccupation with the home was encapsulated in the song 'Home, Sweet Home', the words of which were written by John Howard Payne. This copy of the poem was written by Payne in the album of Lucretia Bates, wife of an American financier resident in London.

British Library, Additional MS. 46132, f. 1

In 1834 a fire (caused by the burning of redundant tally sticks) at the Palace at Westminster destroyed almost all of the magnificent medieval palace except for Westminster Hall. It did however provide the opportunity for a new building to be created to house Britain's Parliament, and 97 architects responded to an invitation to submit designs 'in the Gothic or Elizabethan style'. The winner, Charles Barry, provided the plans and elevations for a lavish Perpendicular Gothic building, and enlisted the assistance of Augustus Pugin to help create the equally ornate design of the interiors. Begun in 1837, the majority of the building work was completed within a decade, but the towers proved more problematical and were still unfinished at the time of Barry's death in 1860, being completed by his son Edward. The Houses of Parliament are a remarkable example of Victorian art and taste, as is demonstrated by this river-front elevation of 1840.

Public Record Office, WORK 29/3203

A separate competition was held for the design and construction of the Palace's great clock, which came to be popularly known as Big Ben, after the chief commissioner of works at the time the clock was installed, Benjamin Hall, Lord Llanover. The maker, E. J. Dent, managed to produce a clock weighing five tons yet keeping time with remarkable accuracy – the dial is illustrated here – but this complex process was not finally completed until 1859.

Public Record Office, WORK 29/3284

Charles Darwin

Charles Darwin (1809–92) was born in Shrewsbury and studied medicine at Edinburgh, but disliked it, describing the lessons as 'cold breakfastless hours on the properties of rhubarb'. He went on to Cambridge instead, becoming friendly with the Professor of Botany there, John Henslow. Henslow arranged for Darwin to join a government expedition to South America on the *H.M.S. Beagle*, which lasted from 1831 to 1836. During the voyage, Darwin was overwhelmed by the impression of the great variety and interdependence of living things, and began to think about how these species came about. On his return to England, he began to sketch his ideas, which resulted in his epoch-making work, *On The Origin of Species*, published in 1859. He argued that the various species had a natural, not divine, origin, and that the necessities of survival had caused creatures to mutate, leading to new species, a process succinctly described by a contemporary as 'survival of the fittest'. In *The Descent of Man* of 1871, he pushed these theories further, proposing that man had evolved from the higher primates. Darwin's theories were inevitably controversial, but they are now at the centre of much modern thought, not only in the natural sciences, but also in social, political and many other forms of study.

Portrait of Charles Darwin in 1886.
Public Record Office, COPY 1/56, f. 767

(right) Title page of the first edition of *On The Origin of Species* (1859).
British Library, C.113.c.8

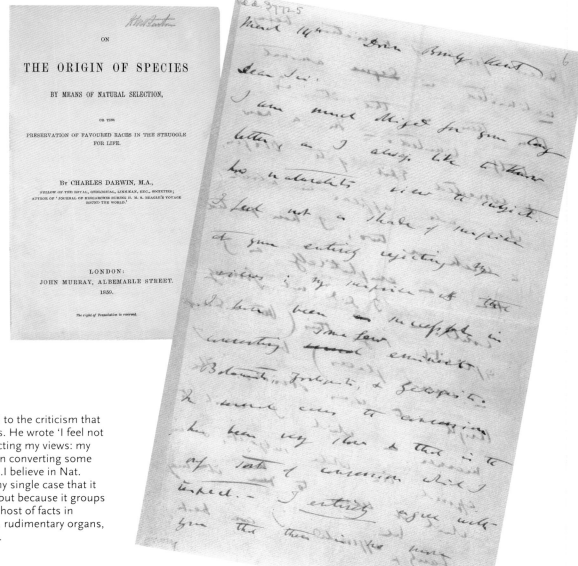

In this letter of 1861, Darwin responded to the criticism that there was no direct proof of his theories. He wrote 'I feel not a shade of surprise at your entirely rejecting my views: my surprise is that I have been successful in converting some few eminent Botanists and Geologists...I believe in Nat. Selection, not because I can prove in any single case that it has changed one species into another, but because it groups and explains well (as it seems to me) a host of facts in classification, embryology, morphology, rudimentary organs, geological succession and distribution'.
British Library, Additional MS. 37725, f.6

Opened by Queen Victoria on 1 May 1851, the Great Exhibition, celebrating trade, manufacturing and industry, was the brainchild of Henry Cole, an Assistant Keeper of Public Records. But this groundbreaking event, the first of the major international trade fairs, was brought to fruition by Prince Albert who chaired the Royal Commission set up to oversee it. The site chosen was Hyde Park in London, where a vast prefabricated iron and glass structure, the Crystal Palace, designed by Sir Joseph Paxton, was erected, over 1,800 feet long and at its broadest 450 feet wide. Within it were housed the extraordinarily diverse displays of 17,000 exhibitors, ranging from engines to textiles to jewels, which were visited by over six million people in less than six months. The Great Exhibition was seen as embodying Britain's 19th-century economic ascendancy and the Victorian belief in trade and enterprise as an instrument of social progress. After its closure the takings of £356,000 were used towards setting up the museums at South Kensington, and the Crystal Palace was moved to Sydenham, where it hosted many more exhibitions, theatrical events and concerts until it was destroyed by fire in 1936.

A series of detailed views of the exhibition was prepared for Prince Albert by three well-known artists, Joseph Nash, Louis Haghe and David Roberts (who was one of the exhibition commissioners). These pictures were published as a souvenir volume of chromolithographs in 1854. Shown here are views of the main transept and of the Tunis Room.
British Library, Cup. 652.c.33

A selection of tickets for the Great Exhibition.
Public Record Office, BT 342/2, after f. 495 and ff 676–7

London's Parks

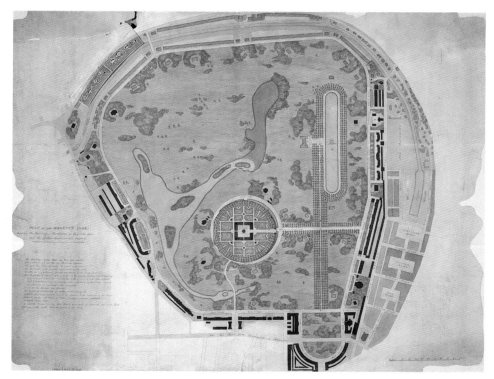

Hyde Park was first opened to the public in the early 17th century, when it was still a royal hunting ground. The largest of London's parks, it has been the haunt of highwaymen; the duelling ground for London society; a site for sculptures, fountains, landscape gardens, art galleries, restaurants. Many major events have been played out in its 340 acres, including a celebratory full-scale re-enactment of the Battle of Trafalgar held in 1814, firework displays, balloon ascents, the Great Exhibition of 1851, and more recently popular open-air concerts. Above all Hyde Park has been a place of fashion, where people have come to see and be seen, as exemplified by this depiction of driving in Hyde Park in 1899.

Public Record Office, COPY 1/154, f. 105

Although part of the Crown lands since the Reformation, Regent's Park was not reclaimed from farmland until 1811. John Fordyce, Surveyor-General of the King's Works, saw the opportunity it offered to enhance the appearance of the increasingly-expanding London and increase the Crown's revenues, and held a competition for the design for a new estate of parkland, villas and terraces. The winner was John Nash, significant parts of whose innovative designs, mixing urban and rural elements, were completed by 1828. One of Nash's designs is illustrated here. Many serious financial problems needed to be solved in creating the park, and only a proportion of Nash's designs were ever built – for example the terraces planned for the northern end of the park were occupied by the zoo instead. The naming of the park after the Prince Regent reflects his personal and unswerving commitment to Nash. By 1841, the public were admitted to the park.

Public Record Office, MPE 912

Florence Nightingale (1820–1910) made her reputation by her organisation of nursing services during the Crimean War. Thereafter she worked tirelessly to improve public health and raise the status of nursing, establishing a school of nursing at St Thomas's Hospital in London.
British Library, Additional MS. 47458, f. 31

On 4 November 1854 Florence Nightingale arrived at Scutari, the former Turkish military barracks which served as a hospital for British troops during the Crimean War. Conditions were already appalling and worsened rapidly as huge numbers of wounded and diseased men arrived at the ill-equipped buildings. From the beginning, Nightingale recognised that her task was not simply to tend to the individual needs of the wounded soldiers, but also to surmount the bureaucratic shortcomings of the army's medical services and to establish a female nursing group which authorities and medical men alike could respect. This letter (left) to Sidney Herbert, her principal supporter in London, deal with her opinions on the status of female nurses and the difficulties caused by the claims of various religious groups to send in parties of women. Nightingale declares that ' The ladies all quarrel among themselves. The Medical Men all laugh at their helplessness but like to have them about for the sake of a little female society'.
British Library, Additional MS. 43393, f. 161v

Elizabeth Fry (right) (1780–1845) was a quaker philanthropist who founded hostels for the homeless and other charities, but is best known for her campaigns to improve prison conditions.
British Library, Additional MS. 47457, f. 2

In 1813, Elizabeth Fry visited Newgate Prison in London, and was horrified by the conditions there. Nearly three hundred women, with their children, were huddled together in two wards 'without employment, without nightclothes or bedclothes, sleeping on the bare floor, cooking and washing, eating and sleeping in the same apartment'. Drinking water came from a single tap. Elizabeth tried to supply the prisoners with clothes, established a school and arranged for the appointment of a matron. In 1817, she helped form an association for the improvement of the prisoners' lot. Her campaign helped bring about legislation leading to a more humane regime in the 1820s and have influenced modern theories on prison management. In this memorandum of 1817 (right), she declares that 'The object of a prison should be to punish & to lessen rather than increase the crimes of the country'.
British Library, Egerton MS. 3673A, f. 100

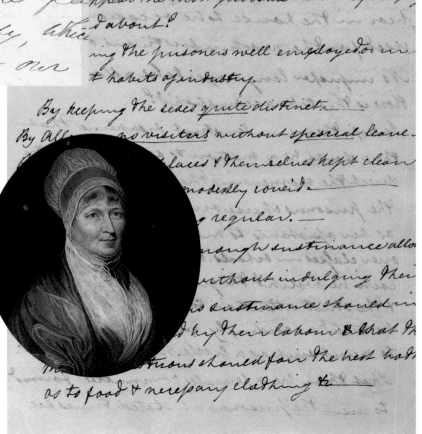

Two Victorian Authors

More famous now as a novelist, Robert Louis Stevenson (1850–94) was also a fine poet in both English and Scots, or Lallans. From his sickly childhood Stevenson remained dogged by serious ill-health. He left Scotland for the life of a wanderer in Europe, America and the South Seas, settling in Samoa, where he became 'Tusitala', Teller of Tales. Today Stevenson's most famous works are his boy's adventure story *Treasure Island* (1883) and the gripping and disturbing story of moral ambiguities *The Strange Case of Dr Jekyll and Mr Hyde* (1886). But perhaps his finest novels took him back to the Scotland of his ancestry, youth and lasting affections: all, like the works of Sir Walter Scott, are enriched by reliance on the Scots language and focus on the tensions between Highland and Lowland or on a society in change. There are *Kidnapped* (1886), its sequel *Catriona* (1893), *The Master of Ballantrae* (1888) and his masterpiece, the unfinished *Weir of Hermiston*. Something of Stevenson's fortitude in the face of persistent illness is conveyed in this early draft of one of his most celebrated poems, 'The Celestial Surgeon', with its moving opening couplet: 'If I have faltered more or less/In my great task of happiness'.

National Library of Scotland, MS. 19637, f. 10

The novels of Charles Dickens (1812–70) achieved during the Victorian period and the early years of this century a canonical status previously only accorded to the Bible, Shakespeare and seminal religious works. A copy of Dickens's works was an indispensable feature of every respectable household. Dickens's novels encapsulate many of the tensions of Victorian society. On the one hand, they look back to the 'Merry England' of coaches and inns. On the other, they are deeply concerned with the moral and social issues posed by a rapidly changing society. Likewise, the epithet 'Dickensian' was applied both to rollicking good humour and to social conditions of dreadful squalor. This is part of Dicken's manuscript of the novel which established his reputation, *Pickwick Papers* (1837).

British Library, Additional MS. 39182, f. 6

Dickens surrounded by famous scenes from his novels.
Public Record Office, COPY 1/563, f. 5878

Edinburgh and Cardiff

In *Marmion*, Walter Scott called his native Edinburgh, 'mine own romantic town'. Almost contemporary with Scott's poem is this watercolour of 1809 by the Irish amateur artist John Harden. Up to the middle years of the 18th century Edinburgh – 'Auld Reekie'– was a famously dirty city confined to the narrow ridge running from the Castle on the west to the Palace of Holyrood on the east. The buildings of the Old Town, which are visible to the left in Harden's picture, were some of the highest in Europe, and were remarkable for the social mix of their inhabitants. From the 1750s progressive men began to think of a new city rising on the open fields beyond the Nor' Loch. William Mylne's North Bridge of 1763, which occupies the centre ground of Harden's drawing, made possible the expansion of the capital. In 1767 James Craig won the competition to plan the layout of a New Town, a grid-iron of streets and squares intended to be a city of reason and enlightenment. To the New Town moved the aristocracy of birth or profession, and the prosperous mercantile classes, leaving the Old Town to become the slum it was until the middle of the 20th century when tourism, the conservation movement and the inherent qualities of the area led to a renaissance.

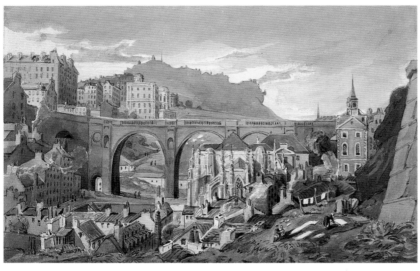

Watercolour view of Edinburgh by John Harden, 1809.
National Library of Scotland, MS. 8868/1

Cardiff Castle and a horse-drawn bus, 1893, from the Francis Frith & Company Collection.
National Library of Wales

Shipping at Bute Docks, Cardiff, 1925.
National Library of Wales

Although the Romans settled in the area of the present city of Cardiff in 75 AD and the Normans constructed one of the finest motte castles in Britain there between 1093 and the late 12th century, Cardiff did not come into its own until the late 19th century. By 1890 Cardiff had surpassed Merthyr and Swansea as the largest town in south Wales. It had become one of the richest and busiest commercial centres in the British Empire because of the huge amounts of coal exported from its docks. The Marquis of Bute had constructed a dock in 1839 and this work continued throughout the 19th century. It was the third Marquis of Bute who employed the architect William Burges to create a great deal of Cardiff Castle and Castell Coch – the fairy-tale hunting lodge among the woods at Tongwynlais on the city's northern fringes. The third Marquis had presented the town with many fine buildings from 1868 onwards and just before his death in 1900 had sold Cathays Park to the corporation for the construction of a fine civic centre worthy of a town whose officials saw themselves as leaders of a Welsh capital. Official recognition of Cardiff as the capital city of Wales, however, was not forthcoming until 1955, an honour granted by the Queen to coincide with the Empire Games which were held in the city that year.

Canada: The First Dominion

Ceded by France to Britain in 1773, Canada remained a British colony after the American War of Independence and became the refuge of exiled loyalists from the United States of America. Canada subsequently became increasingly prosperous but there were tensions and divisions, particularly between the predominantly French-speaking Lower Canada (Quebec) and English-speaking Upper Canada (Ontario). On 1 July 1867, however, Quebec and Ontario were joined by Nova Scotia and New Brunswick in the Dominion of Canada, the first federal union in the British Empire. Ottawa became the federal capital and under Canada's first Prime Minister Sir John MacDonald these states were joined by Manitoba in 1870, British Columbia, to the far west, in 1871 and Prince Edward Island in 1873. By 1885 the Canadian Pacific Railroad linked the country from the Atlantic to the Pacific.

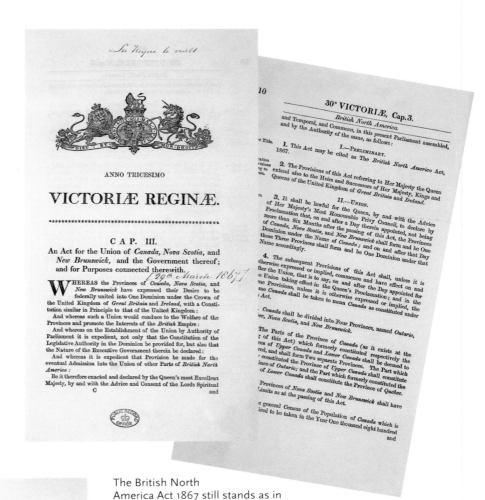

The British North America Act 1867 still stands as in effect Canada's constitution, uniting the states in a federation but safeguarding the language and legal rights of the Francophone population.
Public Record Office, C 65/5336, pages 9–10.

Canada was and remains home to many native peoples, among them the Chippewa or Ojibway of northern Ontario and Lake Superior. The way of life of the Red Lake Chippewas was photographed in 1876 by boundary surveyors working for the North-West Boundary Commission.
Public Record Office, FO 302/30, nos 90 and 92

Victorian politicians appear in retrospect to be almost protean figures, and none more so than two of the outstanding prime ministers from this period, William Ewart Gladstone (1809–98) and Benjamin Disraeli, 1st Earl of Beaconsfield (1804–81). Gladstone began his political life as a high Tory, but became the incarnation of Victorian liberalism whose creed was summed up as 'peace, retrenchment and reform'. Gladstone was strongly committed to free trade, a supporter of nationalist movements in Europe and Ireland, and felt that personal advancement should be on the basis of merit rather than connections. Disraeli sought to breathe new life into the Conservative party after the divisions caused by the campaign to rescind taxes on the import of corn. He considered that the landed classes should exercise a benign paternalism to help curb the worst excesses of industrial society, and favoured strongly the promotion of empire and the extension of British influence overseas.

The personalities of Gladstone and Disraeli also formed a striking contrast. Disraeli had first became famous as the author of satirical novels. He was flamboyant, cynical and wordly-wise, an overt self-promoter. He was, in Gladstone's view, 'not respectable'. Gladstone was driven throughout his careeer by a powerful moral impulse and saw politics as a mission rather than a game. Gladstone was, in Disraeli's view, a tedious windbag. Despite these contrasts and the bitter rivalry between them, both Gladstone and Disraeli played an important part in shaping modern democracy in Britain. Disraeli played a key role in securing the passage of the Reform Act of 1867, which extended the vote to skilled workers. He also helped pioneer modern methods of party political organisation. Gladstone's famous Midlothian Campaign in 1879–80 demonstrated for the first time the political potential of a national leader making a direct appeal to a mass electorate.

A contemporary portrait of Disraeli.
Public Record Office, COPY 1/463, f. 462

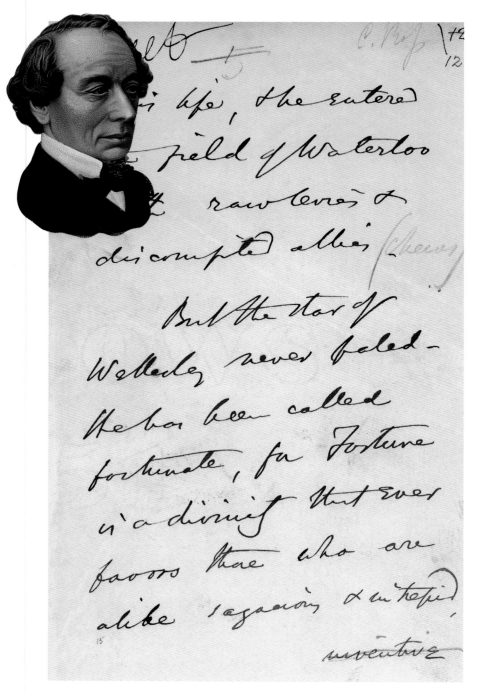

Disraeli was one of the great political stage managers, as can be seen from this draft of his speech at the funeral of the Duke of Wellington in 1852, where he has marked pauses to allow for cheers from the crowds.
British Library, Additional MS. 37502, f. 12

Gladstone and Disraeli

A contemporary portrait of Gladstone.
Public Record Office, COPY 1/38, f. 141

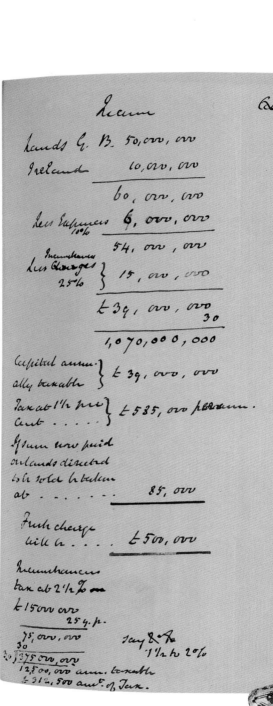

Gladstone was one of the most notable Chancellors of the Exchequer. He sought to implement a programme of free trade, reduced public expenditure and taxes. This reflected a strong moral belief that these measures were necessary to promote self-reliance and hard work, and that they would help promote peace by creating international prosperity and reducing trade disputes. These are some of Gladstone's calculations for his 1853 budget.
British Library, Additional MS. 44741, f. 105

A battered red leather dispatch box used by Gladstone as Chancellor was, until recently, traditionally brought out for the Chancellor on budget day to carry the details of his budget speech to the House of Commons. The present Chancellor prefers to use a new dispatch box, and this Gladstonian relic has reverted to the care of the Public Record Office.

Public Record Office, T 172/1A

England established slave trading posts on the west coast of Africa in the 17th century. English settlers also began to infiltrate the Dutch colony at the Cape of Good Hope, which was finally seized by Britain in 1806. The growth of missionary activity prompted a series of heroic expeditions to explore the interior during the first half of the 19th century, and the continent was regarded as a British sphere of influence, but little formal colonisation occurred. From 1875, other European countries tried to move into Africa, with the French, Belgians and Germans competing with the British to take control of the people and resources of native states, a process that has been called 'The Scramble for Africa'. Britain rapidly annexed large parts of the continent, in an attempt to drive a wedge between its European competitors.

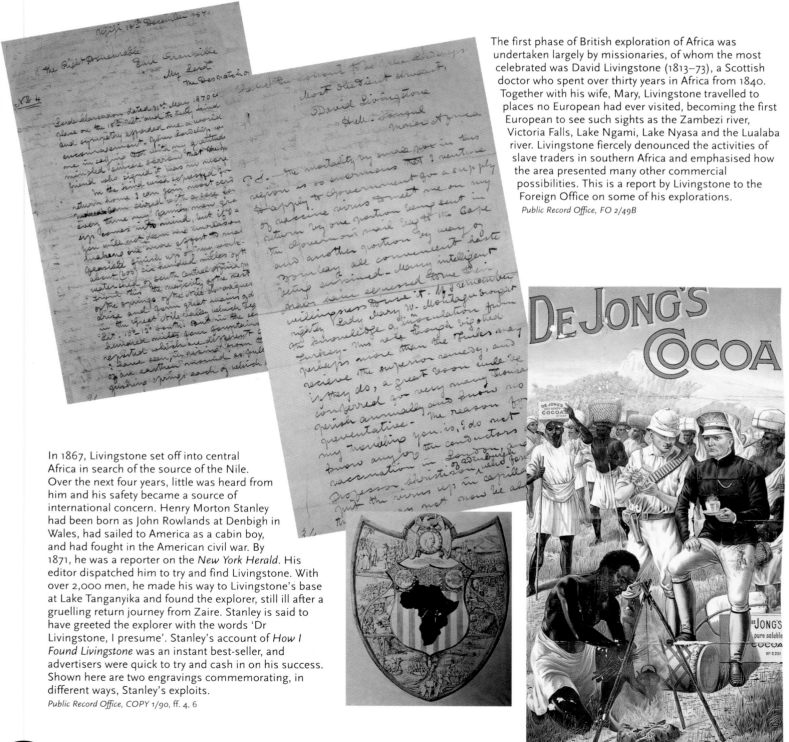

The first phase of British exploration of Africa was undertaken largely by missionaries, of whom the most celebrated was David Livingstone (1813–73), a Scottish doctor who spent over thirty years in Africa from 1840. Together with his wife, Mary, Livingstone travelled to places no European had ever visited, becoming the first European to see such sights as the Zambezi river, Victoria Falls, Lake Ngami, Lake Nyasa and the Lualaba river. Livingstone fiercely denounced the activities of slave traders in southern Africa and emphasised how the area presented many other commercial possibilities. This is a report by Livingstone to the Foreign Office on some of his explorations.
Public Record Office, FO 2/49B

In 1867, Livingstone set off into central Africa in search of the source of the Nile. Over the next four years, little was heard from him and his safety became a source of international concern. Henry Morton Stanley had been born as John Rowlands at Denbigh in Wales, had sailed to America as a cabin boy, and had fought in the American civil war. By 1871, he was a reporter on the *New York Herald*. His editor dispatched him to try and find Livingstone. With over 2,000 men, he made his way to Livingstone's base at Lake Tanganyika and found the explorer, still ill after a gruelling return journey from Zaire. Stanley is said to have greeted the explorer with the words 'Dr Livingstone, I presume'. Stanley's account of *How I Found Livingstone* was an instant best-seller, and advertisers were quick to try and cash in on his success. Shown here are two engravings commemorating, in different ways, Stanley's exploits.
Public Record Office, COPY 1/90, ff. 4, 6

The Scramble for Africa

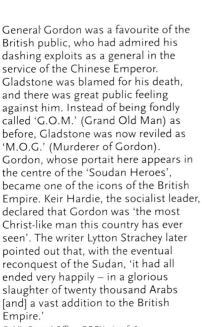

By 1882, Britain was effective ruler of Egypt. In that year, Mohammed Ahmed, known as the Mahdi (one who, according to tradition, would rid the world of evil), led a rebellion against Egyptian rule in the Sudan and defeated the Egyptian army. The British Prime Minister, Gladstone, ordered the Egyptians to abandon Sudan, and dispatched one of the most charismatic British generals, Charles Gordon, to supervise the withdrawal and establish a new government. Gordon had previously been Governor of Sudan, when he had introduced many administrative reforms and reduced the slave trade. Soon after Gordon's arrival in the Sudanese capital Khartoum in February 1884, the city was surrounded by the Mahdi. Gordon asked permission to use the forces of a local slave trader against the Mahdi, but the British government felt this would be too controversial. Gordon made repeated requests for help, but Gladstone, whose instincts were pacifist and anti-imperial, dithered. Despite poor fortifications, lack of food and insufficient soldiers, Gordon withstood the siege for ten months. Gladstone finally sent an expeditionary force to relieve Khartoum; it arrived two days after Khartoum had been taken and Gordon killed. This is the last page of a journal of the siege kept by Gordon on the back of telegraph forms. It ends: 'I have done my best for the honor of our country. C.G. Gordon'. Across the bottom of the page, Gordon has scribbled: 'You send me no information though you have lots of money'.

British Library, Additional MS. 34479, f. 108

General Gordon was a favourite of the British public, who had admired his dashing exploits as a general in the service of the Chinese Emperor. Gladstone was blamed for his death, and there was great public feeling against him. Instead of being fondly called 'G.O.M.' (Grand Old Man) as before, Gladstone was now reviled as 'M.O.G.' (Murderer of Gordon). Gordon, whose portait here appears in the centre of the 'Soudan Heroes', became one of the icons of the British Empire. Keir Hardie, the socialist leader, declared that Gordon was 'the most Christ-like man this country has ever seen'. The writer Lytton Strachey later pointed out that, with the eventual reconquest of the Sudan, 'it had all ended very happily – in a glorious slaughter of twenty thousand Arabs [and] a vast addition to the British Empire.'

Public Record Office, COPY 1/72, f. 69

In 1801, the population of London was just under one million; by 1881, it had quadrupled. Late Victorian London was the largest and wealthiest city in the world. With its underground railways, great department stores, massive docks and advanced sanitation system, it seemed in many respects the city of the future. The city also, however, had a more squalid side.

Many saw it as overwhelmed by countless prostitutes and beggars and as containing many terrible slums where even the police hesitated to venture. In the national folk memory, it is perhaps this darker side of the city which is best remembered. The popular conception of this foggy, gaslit world is epitomised by two figures: Jack the Ripper and Sherlock Holmes.

Between August and November 1888, six women were murdered in a small area of Whitechapel. The bodies of all the victims had been mutilated in a way that led police to conclude that the murderer was a surgeon. Newspapers and the police received taunting notes purporting to be from the murderer, 'Jack the Ripper'. When the police published this facsimile of one of the supposed letters from the murderer, they were overwhelmed by letters from hoaxers claiming to be the culprit. The police never caught the murderer.

Public Record Office, MEPO 3/142

Part of the reason for the popularity of Sir Arthur Conan Doyle's stories of the detective Sherlock Holmes and his friend Dr John Watson was the skill with which Doyle depicted the London of the time. This is an autograph fair copy of 'The Adventure of the Missing Three Quarter', first published in the *Strand Magazine* for August 1904, and reprinted in 1905 in *The Return of Sherlock Holmes*. It was presented to the British Museum on the occasion of the centenary of Doyle's birth. The bookplate of a former owner of the manuscript, Victor Starrett, depicts Holmes in his most famous guise, with deerstalker hat and pipe.

British Library, Additional MS 50065, ff. ii, 2

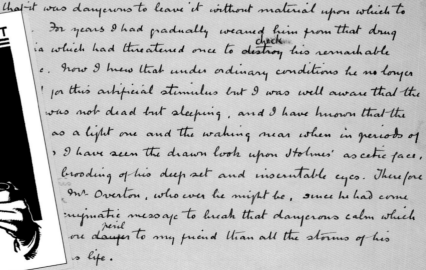

Somdomites and Revolutionaries

Oscar Wilde, the brilliant conversionalist and playwright, was at the height of his fame when he became friendly with Lord Alfred Douglas, the son of the Marquess of Queensbury, the originator of the modern rules of boxing. On 18 February 1895, the Marquess left this visiting card for Wilde at the Albemarle Club in Piccadilly. The (misspelt) message reads 'For Oscar Wilde posing Somdomite', though in court he would claim it read '...posing as a Somdomite'. Wilde unsuccessfully sued the Marquess for libel, and as a result was in turn tried for homosexual acts. This card formed part of the evidence against Wilde. He was found guilty and sentenced to two years' hard labour, emerging a broken man. He spent the rest of his life in Paris, living under the pseudonym Sebastian Melmoth.

Public Record Office, CRIM 1/41/6

The Russian revolutionary Vladimir Il'ich Lenin (1870–1924) and his wife Nadezhda Krupskaya arrived in London in 1902. Like Marx fifty years earlier, Lenin became a reader at the British Museum. This is his letter of application, written under the name of Jacob Richter. Krupskaya writes in her *Memories of Lenin*: 'From the conspiratorial point of view things could not have been better. No identification documents were needed in London then, and one could register under any name. We assumed the name of Richter. Another advantage was that to English people all foreigners looked the same, and our landlady took us for Germans'. Lenin and Krupskaya had taught themselves English in Siberia, where they translated Sidney and Beatrice Webb's *History of Trade Unionism* into Russian.

British Library, Additional MS. 54579, f. 2

Karl Marx (1818–83) was born in Germany and settled in London following the series of revolutions and upheavals in continental Europe in 1848. During his time in England, Marx devoted himself to writing and researching his great work of political philosophy and economy, *Das Kapital*, which was published (in three parts, two of them posthumously) between 1867 and 1894, and worked out in detail Marx's criticism of the capitalist system that the benefits of labour accrued to those who provided the capital rather than those who did the work. Much of Marx's research was done in the British Museum, where a new reading room providing access to a considerably enlarged library had been opened in 1857. This is the Museum's record of the issue of Marx's reading room ticket.

British Library, Additional MS. 54579, f. 1

Tea was introduced to Europe by the Dutch in the 17th century: in 1660, Samuel Pepys saw it as a great rarity. At first imported from China and Japan, it was originally prized for its medicinal properties, but during the 18th century became a fashionable drink. Conditions were favourable for the cultivation of tea in India, and tea-planting was begun there in 1834, extending to Sri Lanka in the 1860s. It was in the 1880s that tea became the British national drink, with brands such as Twining and Lipton being established.

Tea has always been of political importance, whether as a factor in diplomacy with eastern countries or as a major commodity in international trade. Tea was one of the substances which divided England and the United States but helped bond together the economies of the British Empire, as reflected in this poster produced by the Empire Marketing Board.
Public Record Office, CO 956/182

Afternoon tea was established as a social ritual towards the end of the 19th century in order to fill the lengthening hours between lunch and dinner. In Rupert Brooke's poem, 'The Old Vicarage, Grantchester', a powerful expression of nostalgic yearning for the English countryside written in Berlin in 1912, a church clock and afternoon tea become, in the final couplet, the supreme symbols of everything magical about the English countryside and country life: 'Stands the Church clock at ten to three / And is there honey still for tea?' Brooke's poem, the autograph manuscript of which is shown here, was first published during the First World War in 1915, and struck a powerful chord with many of its first readers.
Cambridge, Fitzwilliam Museum

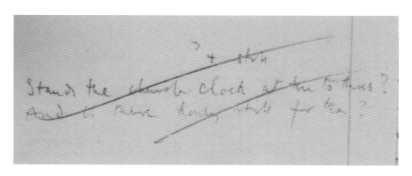

Whisky and Beer

Playing on the life-enhancing properties of its product, this attractive poster for Jacob's Pilsener Lager Beer was registered by Frederick Jacob and Company of Theobald's Road, London on 7 May 1898. The artist was Edwin Hughes.

Successful commercial artists levied high charges for their work, and to protect their investment companies often registered their designs at Stationers' Hall under the Fine Arts Copyright Act 1862. The result was a rich collection of artistic material running up to 1912, now held at the Public Record Office.
Public Record Office, COPY 1/84, f.283

Beer, brewed from barley and hops, was a staple part of the medieval diet and well into the 19th century remained far safer to drink than water. The Beerhouse Act 1830 was an attempt to encourage drinkers of spirits to switch to beer, but resulted in the setting up of 24,000 beerhouses in three months and a great expansion in beer consumption. It had little impact on the sway of gin, until the Licensing Act of 1872, bolstered by the Temperance Movement, sought to regulate the sale of both beer and spirits. Breweries were highly profitable businesses — the flotation of Guinness on the stock market in 1886 was oversubscribed 22-fold and rioters broke down the doors of Barings Bank in their rush for shares.

Whisky, a later and more potent invention, had also become big business by the 1880s and 1890s, when there was a rush to build distilleries in remote Highland areas and then in Tayside, trading on the Glenlivet name. Based on malt and barley and first documented in a Scottish Exchequer roll of 1498 as *aqua vitae*, it was known as *uisgebeatha* in Celtic, from which its Anglicised form, whisky, derived. Distilled at first for the delectation of local Scottish lairds, and soon emulated in Ireland, it did not move into large-scale commercial production until 1830 when the patent still, having originated a few years before, was perfected by an Englishman, Aeneas Coffey, the head of Customs and Excise in Ireland and a talented inventor.

The manufacturers of beer and whisky were heavily dependent on effective advertising to promote their products, and the arrival of the chromolithography process in the 1870s meant that colour posters could be produced cheaply in large numbers from then on.

THE CELEBRATED
BANTASKIN AND "OLD SILENT" MALT LIQUEUR HIGHLAND WHISKIES.

TO BE HAD ONLY FROM B. MACKAY, QUEEN'S BUILDINGS. LENZIE. SCOTLAND

Benjamin Mackay of Lenzie's company and his products were short-lived, but his lively advertisement for Liqueur Highland Whiskies, painted by William McCullum and registered on 17 October 1902, projects an archetypal image of Highland life.
Public Record Office, COPY 1/195,f.159

In the early 19th century, the supposed medical benefits of sea bathing encouraged fashionable society to go to seaside resorts such as Brighton. The development of Wakes' Weeks and similar mill and factory shutdowns in industrial towns provided the working classes with an opportunity to go away, and with the spread of the railways the holidaymakers found that they too could take the sea air. These developments encouraged the growth of Blackpool and other resorts. Legislation for bank holidays was enacted in 1861, which gave a further impetus to the development of the British seaside. Paid holidays gradually became an accepted condition of work. In the 1920s, 1.5 million workers were entitled to paid holidays. By 1939, this figure had risen to 10 million.

Railway companies assiduously promoted the benefits of resorts served by their lines: here the Great Western Railway portrays Tenby as a health resort offering outdoor pursuits. This poster was released in 1905. The artist was Alec Fraser.
Public Record Office, COPY 1/230, f. 202

However, the reality for many British holidaymakers was much rainier, as the artist Henry Tonks found in the 1920s when he took a painting holiday in Kent.
British Library, Additional MS. 46473, f. 75

A Good Sport

Football or soccer as played today across the world is a British invention. Its origins were medieval: whole villages were involved in games with goals many miles apart, and play often became so violent that both the English and Scottish kings periodically banned the game as a threat to public order. Cricket also first appears in the late middle ages: the earliest players were shepherds in south-east England and the name may derive from the Anglo-Saxon *cricc* or shepherd's staff, which was used as the bat. The two 19th-century posters shown here reflect the popularity of both sports and the strong commercial interests associated with them.

Cricket's formal rules were drawn up by the Marylebone Cricket Club (MCC) founded in 1797, and based at Lord's Cricket Ground in London. By the late 19th century, thanks in part to the popularity of the great all-rounder W. G. Grace, it had become England's leading summer sport. In 1909 Australia and South Africa joined England in the Imperial Cricket Conference, later re-named the International Cricket Conference and widened to include India, Pakistan, New Zealand and the West Indies.
Public Record Office, COPY 1/250, f. 65

In the 19th century football too settled down into a more structured pattern: its rules were first codified in 1863 by the Football Association, which launched the FA Cup in 1872. Players were first able to play as professionals in 1885, and three years later the Football League was founded. FIFA, football's international ruling body, was founded in 1904 and has run the World Cup, held every four years and won by England in 1966, since 1930.
Public Record Office, COPY 1/304, f. 296

113

The British Empire reached its greatest extent at the beginning of the 20th century. It was the largest empire the world had ever known, comprising one fifth of the world's land mass and over 400 million people, a quarter of the world's population. However, the Empire had been built up in an extremely haphazard fashion and its organisation was equally *ad hoc*, ranging from dominions such as Canada and Australia to small states controlled directly by the Secretary of State for the Colonies. Politicians were uncertain what to do with the Empire. Some argued that the huge imperial markets could be used to regenerate the British economy. Others saw the Empire as an obstacle to free trade and a drain on the resources of the home country. Perhaps the feelings of pride in seeing so much of the world painted red concealed the truth about the British Empire, that it was really an empire of the sea, which helped ensure supremacy over the sea routes on which the trade and security of the home country depended.

Public Record Office, CO 956/537 (2)

Edward Elgar (1857–1934) was a self-taught composer from Worcester who first achieved fame with his *Enigma Variations*. His *Pomp and Circumstance Marches* were written in 1901, a few days before the death of Queen Victoria, and presumably with an eye to the imminent ceremonies for the accession of Edward VII. This is Elgar's sketch of Pomp and Circumstance March no. 1. In July 1902, a version of the trio section of this march was performed at Covent Garden with words by Arthur Christopher Benson, an archbishop's son and house master at Eton, as a *Coronation Ode*. Shortly afterwards, Benson produced some new words with a longer perspective for Elgar's tune, and *Land of Hope and Glory* was born. On the outbreak of the First World War, Elgar begged that less hysterical words should be used, but the song was too firmly established in popular affection to countenance the composer's plea.

British Library, Additional MS. 47903, f.2

The 20th Century

Beunydd, beunos, y corn rhybudd,
y cyrch disymwth o'r awyr;
try'n oer bob gwefus, arteithia'r llygaid noeth,
try'r cartre'n fedd galarwyr syn.

Alun Llywelyn-Williams, *Rhyngom a Ffrainc*

(Daily, nightly, the warning siren,
the sudden attack from the air;
every lip turns cold, the naked eye becomes tortured,
the home becomes a grave of bewildered mourners.)

The 20th century is an age of paradox. On one hand, it has been hailed as the age of the common man (and woman). The right to vote has been extended to all but a few limited categories of adults. Educational opportunities have been increased and the possibility of a university education is taken for granted. The terrors of poverty through unemployment or ill-health have been ameliorated by state benefits, and the National Health Service makes medical care freely available to everybody. Consumer choice has been extended, and new inventions such as the aeroplane, television and the computer have enriched the quality of life of many.

On the other hand, the 20th century has been scarred by two great wars which dwarfed all previous conflicts. The First World War was seen at first as a war which would end all wars, but came increasingly to be seen as characterised by the pointless squandering of human life by hidebound generals and unimaginative politicians. The aerial combat of the Second World War meant that Britain's cities were brought into the front line and her civilians became as vulnerable as the armed forces. The Cold War brought an even more chilling prospect of eradication of a massive part of the population, a threat which has still not entirely receded with the collapse of the Soviet Union.

At the beginning of the 20th century, Britain still saw itself as the world's leading trading and industrial power, although signs of the future economic superiority of the United States of America, Germany and Japan were already evident. Although Britain is still a leading world economy, the two wars nearly bankrupted the country, much of its manufacturing industry has disappeared and the economy is heavily dependent on the city of London's success as a financial centre. The paradox that after the Second World War Germany and Japan should have prospered while the British economy struggled was difficult for many British people to come to terms with. Yet much of the population experienced a considerable improvement in its standard of living. As Harold Macmillan put it, 'most of our people have never had it so good'.

A London street scene.
Public Record Office, INF3/1738

The 20th century saw the British Empire swell to its greatest extent, then within a short time be reduced to a few small territories. Britain prided itself on the skilful way in which it dismantled the Empire, but the decolonisation process was not always as successful as claimed, as is apparent from the aftermath of the partition of India. The loss of the Empire left Britain uncertain of its role in the world. It remained consistently sceptical and uncertain in its relations with the growing Common Market (now the European Union), finally taking the plunge of membership in 1973 in a very gingerly fashion.

Perhaps the most striking feature of 20th-century Britain has been the way in which its constituent nations have reasserted their identity. In Wales, the movement for greater recognition for the Welsh language resulted in Welsh recovering its status as a legal language after over 400 years. In Scotland, the demands for greater devolution of power culminated in the revival of the Scottish parliament. Again, however, there is a paradox. Despite the attempts to preserve Welsh, Gaelic and other languages of Britain, English at the end of the 20th century continues to sweep all before it, and looks set to become the new world language. At the same time, Britain has become increasingly a cosmopolitan and multi-cultural society. The British inheritance down the ages reflects the accommodation reached between the different peoples of the island. The nature of the British inheritance in the new millennium will reflect new ways of living together that they are currently working out.

When she sailed on her maiden voyage from Southampton, bound for New York, RMS *Titanic* was already the most famous ship of her day: the largest passenger steamer ever built, a by-word for opulence and luxury, capable of the very fast top speed of 24 knots under full steam, and – because of her sixteen transverse bulkheads extending well above her waterline – seen as unsinkable. This photograph of her shows her distinctive four funnels, three linked to the great boilers deep in her hull. Her lifeboats could hold 1178 people, but her passengers and crew numbered 2,228 as she left her last post of call, Queenstown (now Cobh) in Ireland, on 11 April 1912. By the early hours of 15 April she had collided with an iceberg and foundered in an icy-cold sea in the north Atlantic, with the loss of 1,523 people, 815 passengers and 688 crew. This, one of the worst maritime disasters of the 20th century, has haunted the public imagination ever since.
Public Record Office, COPY 1/566

An early indication of trouble came when at 11.45 the wireless operator of the Russian steamer SS *Birma* intercepted a distress call from 'MGY', the call-sign of *Titanic*, telling him that the great liner, 100 miles to his north and well out of reach of help, had struck an iceberg and was sinking. By 1.40 am on 12 April the stricken ship sent out its final distress call, including the new international code SOS. This copy of the telegram was later obtained by the Board of Trade from its diplomatic contacts in St Petersburg.
Public Record Office, MT 9/920, no 6

A sample page from the official list of passengers presumed drowned gives the names of some of the people in first class, showing that death was no respecter of rank. It includes the *Titanic*'s designer, Thomas Andrews; Major Archibald Butt, an advisor of President Taft; and one of the richest men in the world, John Jacob Astor. Despite these losses, 62% of first class passengers were saved but 62% of third class passengers, emigrants from all over Europe seeking a new life in America, were drowned. So shocking was the scale of the disaster that both the British and American governments ordered formal enquiries to be held, and in 1913 an International Conference on the Safety of Life at Sea established an international ice patrol and rules for the adequate provision of lifeboats on ocean-going vessels.
Public Record Office, BT 100/260

Scott of the Antarctic

In January 1902, the National Antarctic Expedition, commanded by a young naval officer, Robert Falcon Scott (1868–1912), arrived in the Ross Sea aboard the *Discovery*. During the next two years, Scott and his companions gathered much new scientific information about Antarctica and made the first long journey into the interior of the continent. On his return to Britain, Scott announced his intention of organising another expedition which would reach the South Pole. He returned to the Antarctic in 1911 to find that the Norwegian explorer Amundsen was also preparing an attempt on the Pole. Scott and his men considered some of Amundsen's methods ungentlemanly. Amundsen's expedition would eat their sleigh dogs and use them as food for other dogs, a practical measure which reduced weight and avoided the scurvy which had frequently hampered the British. Scott was willing to eat his ponies, but drew the line at his dogs. Scott experimented with motorised sledges, but when these broke down the party resorted to the 'more noble' practice of man-hauling sledges. Scott reached the South Pole on 18 January 1912, only to find that Amundsen had got there three days earlier. Hampered by appalling weather and inadequate food supplies, but glorified by acts of great heroism and *sang froid*, Scott and his men perished on the return journey.

The party which reached the South Pole. They are, from left to right: Captain Lawrence Oates, who sacrificed his life to save his colleagues, walking out of the tent into a blizzard with the famous words 'I am just going outside and may be some time'; Lieutenant Henry Bowers, whose last-minute addition by Scott to the party added to the strain on the expedition's inadequate food supplies; Scott; Edward Wilson, a scientist who had been with Scott on his earlier expedition; and Petty Officer Edgar Evans, the first to die on the return journey. This is one of the photographs retrieved from Scott's tent after his death.
British Library, Additional MS. 51042, f. 1

The cover of *The South Polar Times*, a magazine compiled for the expedition's entertainment by Apsley Cherry-Garrard, its assistant zoologist.
British Library, Additional MS. 51040, f. 1

Scott's last letter was addressed to his friend J. M. Barrie, the author of *Peter Pan* . Scott begins with typical understatement: 'We are pegging out in a very comfortless spot'. He goes on to express his sadness that there had been some cooling in their friendship, and assures Barrie of his continued affection.
British Library, Additional MS.46272, f. 1

Gerturude Jekyll (1843–1932) was one of the most influential of all English gardeners. She studied at the Kensington School of Art where she met John Ruskin and William Morris. Learning after her father's death that she was suffering from progressive myopia, she was forced to give up painting and embroidery and devoted herself to garden design. Working closely with the architect Edward Lutyens (who called her 'Aunt Bumps'), she developed a new approach to garden design which was influenced by cottage gardening and attempted to bring an artistic appreciation of colour to gardening. She designed over 300 gardens, and popularised her ideas through her numerous publications. These illustrations are taken from her books, *Children and Gardens* (1908) and *Gardens for Small Country Houses* (1912).

British Library, 7030.w.1; 07031.f.20

Percy Aldridge Grainger (1882–1961), born in Melbourne, was a youthful piano virtuoso who became a friend of the Norwegian composer Edvard Grieg. He settled in London in 1901, at a time when the folk songs of English rural society were in danger of disappearing. Grainger was one of a number of composers who transcribed these songs, recording them for posterity, and made use of them for their own arrangements and compositions. His most famous folk song arrangement is *Country Gardens*, the opening page of which is shown here. Grainger pointed out that many English country gardens are vegetable plots, and that, when playing the arrangement, the performer should have in mind a vigorous gardening activity, like digging turnips.

British Library, Additional MS. 50823, f. 5

Votes for Women

New No. 728.
Old No. 6.

Reference to Papers.

Corres

770809

Metropolitan Police.

Lee Road STATION   A   DIVISION.

5th June 1913

With reference to attached Correspondence I beg to report that at about 3pm on 4th inst I was on duty on Epsom Race Course when the race for the Derby Stakes took place.

When the horses were rounding Tattenham Corner Miss Emily Davison, a well known militant Suffragette suddenly rushed from under the rail immediately in front of "Amner" a horse owned by H.M. The King, and ridden by Herbert Jones.

The woman was knocked down and rendered unconscious, the horse was thrown down and the Jockey also rendered unconscious.

Police of "K" Division were on duty at the spot and PS 4th Bunn 8th Burridge and PC 59th Eady promptly went to the assistance of [...] and Insp White [...] PC 50th Brown, & 85th Johnson

300000-4-12   M.P. 19 & 24b

Beware! The destruction of property is but the beginning.

(left) Between 1886 and 1911 Parliament repeatedly defeated bills to give the vote or suffrage to women, and the Suffragettes – the name was coined by a *Daily Mail* journalist – sought to realise their goal of votes for women by a militant and high profile campaign, launched in 1906 by Emmeline Pankhurst and her daughters. The Suffragettes chained themselves to railings, opted out of paying taxes, interrupted political meetings, and in 1913 attempted to blow up the house of Lloyd George, at that time Chancellor of the Exchequer. In the same year, Emily Davison threw herself under the hooves of the king's horse at the Derby, Britain's leading horserace, and was killed. This is a police report on the incident.
Public Record Office, MEPO 2/1551, f. 6

(above) Many Suffragettes went on hunger strike when in prison, and could be released and then re-arrested when they had recovered their strength. Fanny Parker, alias Janet Arthur, a niece of Lord Kitchener, was arrested in July 1914 for attempting to blow up Burns' Cottage in Alloway and is shown here being led away by the police. For four days she was forcibly fed, a punishment only introduced into Scotland that year, and an experience she later described as 'deliberate cruelty'.
National Archives of Scotland, HH16/43

(left) A postcard addressed 'To British Tyrants: Asquith and Co' illustrates the Suffragettes turn to more militant action.
National Archives of Scotland, JC26/1551

The First World War saw the suspension of the Suffragettes' campaign, and the bringing in for the first time of large numbers of women into occupations previously reserved only for men: this was key to eroding opposition to female suffrage. In 1918 women over 30 years old were given the vote and ten years later this was extended to all women over 21 years old.

The outbreak of the First World War was greeted with great enthusiasm by many citizens of the belligerent countries. In Britain hundreds of thousands of young men volunteered for the Army during the first weeks of the war. This excitement soon turned to disillusionment as stalemate developed on the Western Front and casualties mounted. British society was transformed by the demands of total war. The energies of the civilian population were mobilised and directed in a way which would have been inconceivable before 1914.

Photograph of British tank undergoing trials in 1917. The development of the tank, or land ship as it was initially known, was an attempt to break out of the stalemate of the Western Front. Although initially successful in battle the tank was not produced in sufficient numbers to make a real impact.
Public Record Office, MUN 5/394 no WAT 24

As the result of manpower shortages, women were increasingly recruited to do work traditionally undertaken by men. Here, below, a woman employed by the Lancashire and Yorkshire Railway in 1917 cleans lamps and attends to incandescent burners. Women bore the brunt of hardships at home. As a mark of respect for their contribution, women over 30 were granted the vote in 1918.
Public Record Office, RAIL 343/725 no 22

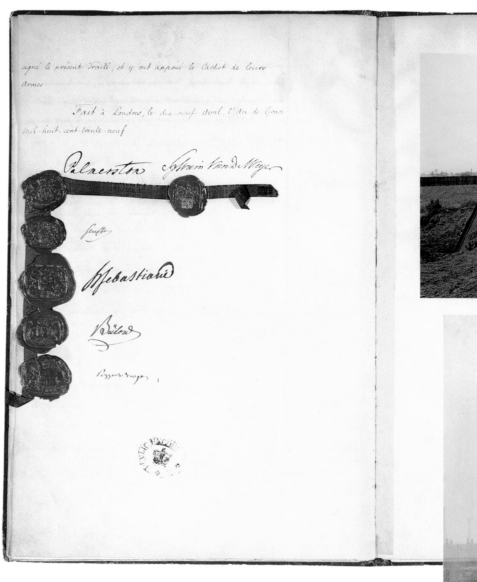

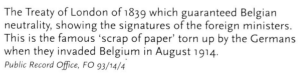

The Treaty of London of 1839 which guaranteed Belgian neutrality, showing the signatures of the foreign ministers. This is the famous 'scrap of paper' torn up by the Germans when they invaded Belgium in August 1914.
Public Record Office, FO 93/14/4

WAR DIARY
or
INTELLIGENCE SUMMARY.
(Erase heading not required.)

Army Form C. 2118.

Instructions regarding War Diaries and Intelligence Summaries are contained in F. S. Regs., Part II. and the Staff Manual respectively. Title pages will be prepared in manuscript.

Hour, Date, Place	Summary of Events and Information	Remarks and references to Appendices
Oct. 31 HOLLEBEKE	As the day went on, shelling became steadily heavier. Machine-guns were destroyed, Capts North and Hunt killed. All the damage was done in trenches provided with overhead cover. Narrow trenches without parapets were immune. A Sqdn on our right, opp. large Chateau, was under heavy sniping but little shell fire. After heaviest possible shelling a strong infantry attack developed from the village and we called in French to strengthen trenches. 2 Sqdns 1st Life Guards also arrive. Hostile infantry seem much surprised at coming under heavy fire at about 700x range, lose heavily and fail to make any ground. At 9 pm we withdrew to ST ELOI. There was heavy sniping there, so had no billets. went on to VOORMEZEELE and bivouacked there.	Killed. Officers. Captain. F.W. Hunt. Capt. K.C. North. men 7838 Pte Reeves. 9777 " Byrne. 4539 Sergt Minton. Wounded. 825 Corpl Galvin. 10096 Pte Rowan. 4461 Corpl Beardow. 8148 Pte Hunt. 9360 Sergt Raywood. 9257 L Cpl Lynch. 6684 Corpl Hall. 2268 Pte Warnock. 6686 " Nolan. 10066 " Peale. 6576 " Crispin. 11473 " Stone. 4253 " Keene. 4473 " Turpin. 1056 " Hillier. 10223 " Hawkshaw. 4817 " Wright.
Nov 1. E of KEMMEL	At 6 am marched to KEMMEL, leaving heavy fight on our left for WYTSCHAETE. Sent out from KEMMEL to cover detachments of our troops retiring, enemy having rushed WYTSCHAETE. At 11 am German advance stopped. Regiment remained in position. A Sqdn joining up. At dusk ordered to outpost line but French took over at 11 pm and we went into neighbouring farms for the night	

For the Fallen.

With proud thanksgiving, a mother for her children,
England mourns for her dead across the sea.
Flesh of her flesh they were, spirit of her spirit,
Fallen in the cause of the free.

Solemn the drums thrill. Death august and royal
Sings sorrow up into immortal spheres.
There is music in the midst of desolation,
And a glory that shines upon our tears.

They went with songs to the battle, they were young,
Straight of limb, true of eye, steady & aglow:
They were staunch to the end against odds uncounted,
They fell with their faces to the foe.

They shall grow not old, as we that are left grow old;
Age shall not weary them nor the years condemn.
At the going down of the sun and in the morning
We will remember them.

They mingle not with their laughing comrades again;
They sit no more at familiar tables of home;
They have no lot in our labour of the day-time;
They sleep beyond England's foam.

But where our desires are, and our hopes profound,
Felt like a well-spring that is hidden from sight,
To the innermost heart of their own land they are known
As the stars are known to the Night;

As the stars that shall be bright when we are dust,
Moving in marches upon the heavenly plain;
As the stars that are starry in the time of our darkness
To the end, to the end they remain.

Laurence Binyon.

The entry for the 4th Hussars for 22 August 1914 describing one of the first encounters between British and German forces on the outskirts of Mons in Belgium. The diary notes that information about enemy positions was obtained by telephoning neighbouring villages.
Public Record Office, WO 95/1134

The poet and art historian Laurence Binyon worked successively in the Department of Printed Books and the Department of Prints and Drawings at the British Museum, and in 1913 was placed in charge of the Museum's collection of oriental prints and drawings. During the First World War, he served with a Red Cross unit in France. This is Binyon's autograph manuscript of 'For the Fallen', perhaps his most important poem, first published in *The Times* on 21 September 1914. Even today it is often recited at remembrance services.
British Library, Additional MS. 45160, f. 1

Ever since the Armistice in 1918 the heroism of the millions of men who lost their lives has attracted great admiration but also, increasingly, deep regret that their sacrifice seemed in vain: so little was settled at the Treaty of Versailles in 1919 that twenty years later the world was to go back to war again.

In Britain the war had exposed the weakness of the country's position as the leading world power and created a lasting mood of cynicism and disillusionment.

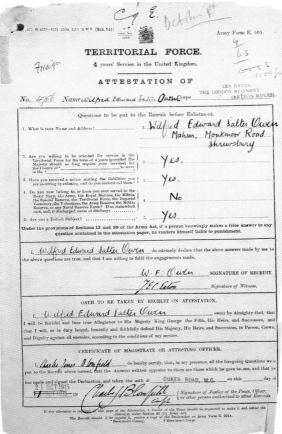

The poet Wilfred Owen served with the Manchester Regiment, having enlisted in 1915. This is his service record. Owen won a Military Cross for conspicuous gallantry. Tragically he was killed in action on 4 November 1918, just a week before the Armistice. The surviving records for British combatants who served in the First World War are now largely at the Public Record Office.
Public Record Office, WO 138/74

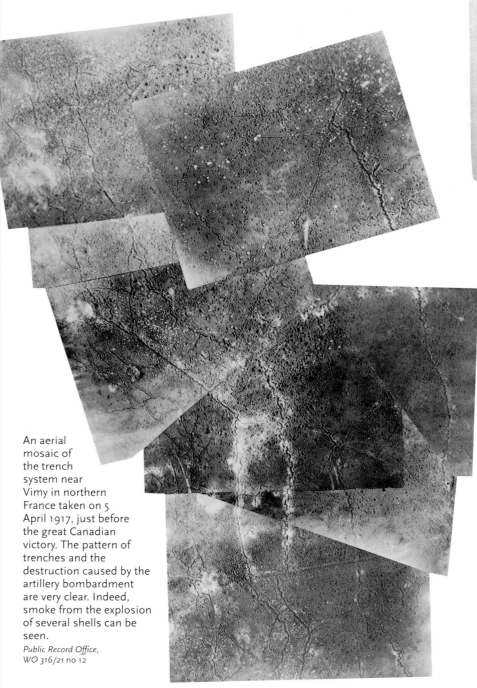

An aerial mosaic of the trench system near Vimy in northern France taken on 5 April 1917, just before the great Canadian victory. The pattern of trenches and the destruction caused by the artillery bombardment are very clear. Indeed, smoke from the explosion of several shells can be seen.
Public Record Office, WO 316/21 no 12

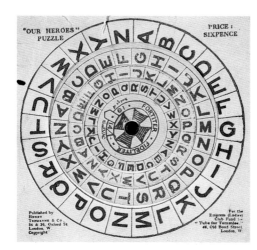

Anagram game sold in aid of the 'Tubs for Tommies Fund', one of the thousands of charities established to provide comforts for British and Allied troops. Unfortunately the game did not prove popular with the public and the promoters made a large loss.
Public Record Office, MEPO 2/1732

'Dulce et Decorum est'

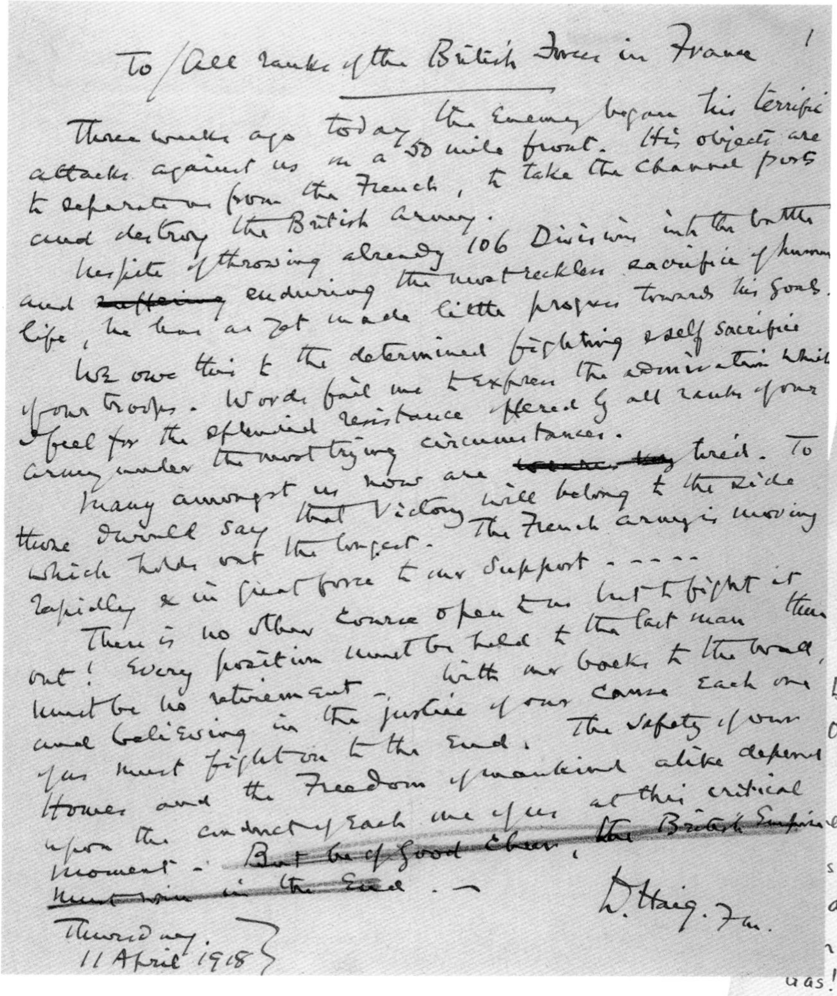

To / All ranks of the British Forces in France

[Haig's handwritten order - partially legible]

Three weeks ago today, the enemy began his terrific
attacks against us on a 50 mile front. His objects are
to separate us from the French, to take the Channel ports
and destroy the British army.

Despite of throwing already 106 Divisions into the battle
and enduring the most reckless sacrifice of human
life, he has as yet made little progress towards his goals.

We owe this to the determined fighting & self sacrifice
of our troops. Words fail me to express the admiration which
I feel for the splendid resistance offered by all ranks of our
army under the most trying circumstances.

Many amongst us now are tired. To
those I would say that Victory will belong to the side
which holds out the longest. The French army is moving
rapidly & in great force to our support ——

There is no other course open to us but to fight it
out! Every position must be held to the last man and
must be no retirement. With our backs to the wall,
and believing in the justice of our cause each one
of us must fight on to the end. The safety of our
Homes and the Freedom of mankind alike depend
upon the conduct of each one of us at this critical
moment. But be of Good Cheer, the British Empire

D. Haig. F.M.

Thursday
11 April 1918

(left) On 21 March 1918, the Germans launched a massive
attack, forcing the British and their allies to retreat. On 11
April, the Commander in Chief of the British Expeditionary
Force in France, General Sir Douglas Haig, issued this order
of the day, which became known as the 'Backs to the Wall'
message, and was intended to restore shaken morale
among the troops under Haig's command. The British
victories in the summer and autumn of 1918, although now
almost forgotten, were among the greatest ever achieved by
the British army.
British Library, Additional MS. 45416, f. 1

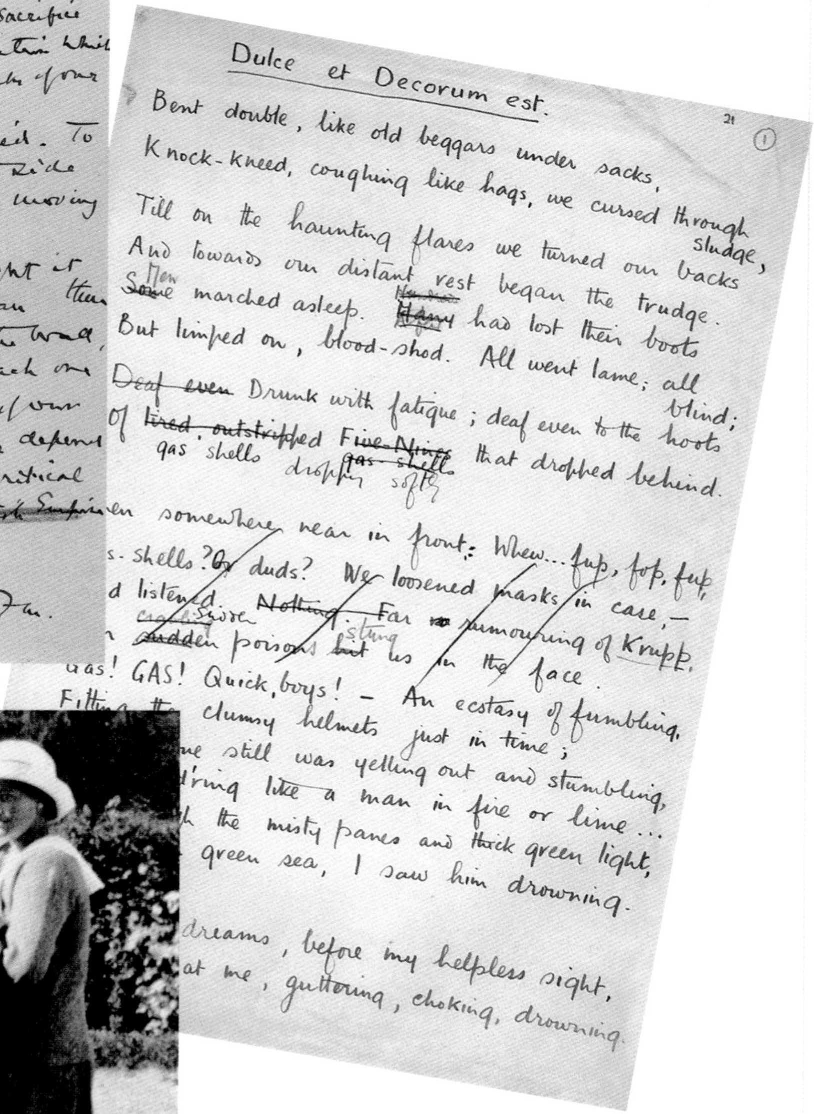

Dulce et Decorum est.

Bent double, like old beggars under sacks,
Knock-kneed, coughing like hags, we cursed through sludge,
Till on the haunting flares we turned our backs
And towards our distant rest began the trudge.
Men marched asleep. Some had lost their boots
But limped on, blood-shod. All went lame; all blind;
Drunk with fatigue; deaf even to the hoots
Of tired, outstripped Five-Nines that dropped behind.
gas shells dropping softly

Gas! Gas! Quick, boys! — An ecstasy of fumbling,
Fitting the clumsy helmets just in time;
But someone still was yelling out and stumbling,
And flound'ring like a man in fire or lime...
Dim, through the misty panes and thick green light,
As under a green sea, I saw him drowning.

In all my dreams, before my helpless sight,
He plunges at me, guttering, choking, drowning.

(above) Wilfred Owen is now universally regarded as
the most important of the war poets, although few of
his poems were published during the war itself. This
is the autograph manuscript of one of his most vivid
and biting poems, 'Dulce et Decorum Est', which was
written a few weeks before his death. The title refers
to an old motto, 'It is sweet and fitting to lay down
one's life for one's country'.
British Library, Additional MS. 43720, f. 21

The last known photograph of Emperor Nicholas II of Russia, taken with one of his guards
at Ekaterinburg a few days before Nicholas was murdered by the Bolsheviks on 16 July 1918.
Public Record Office, FO 371/3977 pt 2, f65

The name of Lawrence of Arabia is synonymous with romantic heroism, but many people are uncertain exactly what Lawrence did and why he was important. Thomas Edward Lawrence (1888–1935) was an archaeologist working on a British Museum expedition in the Middle East when the First World War started. The Middle East was at that time under the rule of the Ottoman Empire, which entered the war as an ally of Germany and Austria. Lawrence joined British military intelligence in Egypt. In 1916, his group incited a rebellion by the Arabs against the Turks, and Lawrence was appointed special advisor to Prince Faisal, the Arab military leader. Through his understanding of Arab culture and society, Lawrence quickly won the confidence and

respect of Faisal and his tribal levies. Lawrence's 'tip and run' tactics proved brilliantly effective, and by 1917 much of the area which is now Saudi Arabia was under joint Arab-British control. Lawrence linked up with the British expeditionary force, and in 1918 he led Arab troops into Damascus. Declaring that his motto was 'Never outstay a climax', he then returned home, where he wrote an account of his adventures, *The Seven Pillars of Wisdom* (1926), which was immediately hailed as a classic, although it was also criticised for exaggerating Lawrence's own role in events. He advised the Colonial Office on middle eastern policy, but then changed his name to Shaw by deed poll and joined the Royal Air Force as an ordinary aircraftman. He was killed in a motor cycle accident at the age of 46 in 1935.

A page from Lawrence's campaign diary for 19 February 1917. Supplies were often a problem for the Arab forces. Lawrence notes that 'Feisul sent a request to Boyle that at Dhaba he should be a little more sparing of the shells, since he had put them to considerable expense at Wejh'.
British Library, Additional MS. 45914, f. 22

Lawrence started assuming Arab dress and eating Arab food before the First World War while he was working on the British Museum expedition excavating the Hittite city of Carchemish. These years were, Lawrence afterwards said, 'the best life I ever lived'.
British Library, Additional MS. 41178, f. 3

Balfour and Palestine

The 'Balfour Declaration' is a fundamental document in the history of the state of Israel. As Foreign Secretary, Balfour wrote on 2 November 1917 to the British Zionist leader Lord Rothschild declaring that the British government would use its best endeavours to establish a national home for the Jewish people in Palestine, subject to the rights of existing non-Jewish communities in Palestine. The terms of this declaration were incorporated into Britain's mandate from the League of Nations for the administration of Palestine after the First World War, and it helped make Palestine the focus of settlement by European Jewish refugees between the wars. Nevertheless, the declaration came in for criticism. It was alleged that it was a manoeuvre to obtain American support in the First World War, and also that it was used to prevent Jewish immigration to Britain and elsewhere. It was pointed out that Balfour himself had been a prominent supporter of the Alien Immigration Act of 1905 which had restricted Jewish immigration into Britain.

British Library, Additional MS. 41178, f. 3

Arthur Balfour (1848–1930), shown below centre, putting, in 1888, owed his political rise to his uncle the Conservative Prime Minister Lord Salisbury. Balfour was Secretary for Ireland from 1887–91, and ascended to the leadership of the Conservative Party, finally becoming Prime Minister in 1902. Balfour's government passed an important Education Act, but Balfour was unable to control the splits in his party over trade policy, and the Conservatives were massively defeated by the Liberals in 1906, Balfour himself losing his parliamentary seat. Quickly returned to parliament by another constituency, Balfour was not highly rated as leader of the opposition and resigned as party leader in 1911. On the outbreak of the First World War, he joined the coalition government as First Lord of the Admiralty and afterwards Foreign Secretary. He was a British delegate at the Versailles peace conference after the First World War and represented Britain at the first assembly of the League of Nations.

Public Record Office, COPY 1/392

Foreign Office,
November 2nd, 1917.

Dear Lord Rothschild,

I have much pleasure in conveying to you, on behalf of His Majesty's Government, the following declaration of sympathy with Jewish Zionist aspirations which has been submitted to, and approved by, the Cabinet.

"His Majesty's Government view with favour the establishment in Palestine of a national home for the Jewish people, and will use their best endeavours to facilitate the achievement of this object, it being clearly understood that nothing shall be done which may prejudice the civil and religious rights of existing non-Jewish communities in Palestine, or the rights and political status enjoyed by Jews in any other country".

I should be grateful if you would bring this declaration to the knowledge of the Zionist Federation.

INSTRUMENT OF ABDICATION

I, Edward the Eighth, of Great Britain, Ireland, and the British Dominions beyond the Seas, King, Emperor of India, do hereby declare My irrevocable determination to renounce the Throne for Myself and for My descendants, and My desire that effect should be given to this Instrument of Abdication immediately.

In token whereof I have hereunto set My hand this tenth day of December, nineteen hundred and thirty six, in the presence of the witnesses whose signatures are subscribed.

SIGNED AT
FORT BELVEDERE
IN THE PRESENCE
OF

Edward RI

Albert

Henry.

George.

The eldest son of King George V, Edward VIII succeeded his father in January 1936. Within a year, on 11 December 1936, he had renounced his throne, days before his planned coronation. When in November the King had announced that he intended to marry his longstanding mistress, Wallis Simpson, an American citizen who was already twice divorced, the Conservative Prime Minister of the day, Stanley Baldwin, argued that this was incompatible with his role of Supreme Head of the Church of England. Baldwin refused Edward a legislative solution: abdication or renunciation of Mrs Simpson were the stark alternatives on offer. Edward chose the woman he loved before the throne and went into exile in France where the pair were married in June 1937, taking the title of Duke and Duchess of Windsor.

Edward's terse and brief Instrument of Abdication, signed by him and his brothers, irrevocably renouncing the throne for him and his descendants, gives little idea of the constitutional turmoil into which he had plunged his country.
Public Record Office, PC 11/1

During Edward's brief period as King, only one set of four stamps were issued for Great Britain. Essays for stamp issues in the Empire and Commonwealth were prepared, but not issued.
British Library, Philatelic Collections

This letter written by the former Liberal Prime Minister David Lloyd George, to his son Gwilym, analysing the abdication, by contrast gives a fascinating insight into the author's relationship with Edward VIII and his view of Baldwin's true role in the crisis. An ardent Welshman, Lloyd George had been instrumental in creating the young Edward Prince of Wales in 1910, and supported him as a liberaliser; but he thought that Baldwin had flattered and cajoled a weak and foolish Labour Party into helping him remove the king because they all feared Edward's democratic tendencies.
National Library of Wales, NLW MS 23654, f. 10

The Beeb

Established in 1922 as a private company, the BBC or British Broadcasting Company became the British Broadcasting Corporation in 1927 when it was converted to a public body by royal charter, the world's first public-service broadcasting organisation. By this time it had already outgrown its first premises at Savoy Hill, off the Strand. Broadcasting House, situated just north of Oxford Street, was designed by G. Val Myer and opened in 1932. It contained 22 studios, including a concert hall, a hall for public debates and special studios for religious services, dance music, military music and vaudeville programmes.
British Library, 08755.dd.53, frontispiece

Much of the BBC's standing stems from its high technical standards. This 1937 postcard shows the west regional medium wave transmitter, part of a network established by the BBC in the late 1920s to ensure that all listeners could receive two radio programmes, one national and one regional.
British Library, W.P. 11152

But above all the BBC's reputation was founded on its political impartiality and its public service ethos; both were laid down by the first Director-General, John Reith (1922–38). The cornerstone of the BBC's public service ethos was its monopoly, preserved by regularly renewed royal charter, and the system of finance whereby licences were required for every radio and television set. The Attlee government set up in 1946 a commission of inquiry which vindicated this arrangement, and the BBC charter was duly renewed in 1952 and enrolled on the Patent Roll, shown here. Nevertheless, four years later the BBC's monopoly was to be broken when a commercial television service was started.
Public Record Office, C 66/5490, no 8.

An Empire Service of the BBC was established at Lord Reith's behest in 1932. It was intended to keep the king's loyal subjects in touch with the mother country, and the idea of foreign language broadcasting was abhorred in case it prejudiced the integrity of the service. Foreign language services were introduced from 1938 in response to propaganda from Germany, Italy and elsewhere, and burgeoned during the war. After the war, the value of the BBC's independent and objective news service as the Cold War developed was widely appreciated, but the service was constantly at risk from government parsimony. Services to the Soviet Union were begun in 1947, but were jammed from 1949. This Foreign Office minute of 1952 illustrates the complex diplomatic and technical issues raised by broadcasts to Eastern Europe and the constant threat of Soviet jamming.
Public Record Office, FO 953/1292

Britain had drifted into the Second World War almost as unprepared as she had been a generation before. Her leaders believed that war would again be the static affair it had been between 1914 and 1918. It was to be very different. The brilliantly executed German offensive through the Ardennes and then the Blitz over London in 1940 proved this. For a year between June 1940 and June 1941 Britain, and her Commonwealth allies, faced the might of Nazi Germany alone. Then, and in the years to follow, Britain prepared for the invasion of the Continent, which eventually came in June 1944.

Report of an attack on a German E-Boat between Calais and Dunkirk on 12 January 1941 by Squadron Leader Douglas Bader, DSO, DFC. Bader was famous for flying without legs, following their amputation, and became one of the most decorated pilots of the War. This was all in a days work for 242 Squadron based at Mildenhall, Suffolk.
Public Record Office, AIR 50/92 f19

- 2 -   **19**

Off Dyck Lightship when P/O Edmonds was warned of the Me.109 he orbitted, when suddenly he met E/A in cloud in head-on attack. He fired without noticing result but received a cannon hit 6" off outside port gun without knowing been hit. He orbitted for a considerable time but could find no trace so he returned to base, making landfall at Folkestone. Following the landed Martlesham 15.10.

The three pilots report sighting what appeared to be a warship to the of Dunkirk.

All pilots report concentrated and accurately predicted Flak bursting front of our aircraft and principally situated round Dunkirk.

Weather: Cloud 1 to 1500 ft. 7/10ths. Visibility good below cloud.

Our Casualties: 1A/C Cat. 1
F/O McKnight D.F.C. and P/O Latta, D.F.C. have not returned to base by 17.00 hours, and are presumed missing.

                                     R. Barrington (sgd.)
                                           F/Lt.
                        Station Intelligence Officer.

Patrol No. 1. 1020 - 1135 hours

S/Ldr. Bader and F/Lt. Turner crossed coast 2 miles N. of Felixstowe and set course for French coast at 1020 hours.

Clouds 800 feet at coast. On the way over the sea, clouds varied between 400 and 800 feet. Bad visibility necessitated turning S.W. to obtain position and Ramsgate (North Foreland) was sighted. Course then set for some point E. of Calais.

French coast sighted from 2 miles distant at 600 feet, and we turned and flew E 2 miles out. At about midway between Dunkirk and Calais 2 small naval vessels were sighted ½ mile out from coast, proceeding Eastwards. Turned about one mile ahead of them, and proceeded in a shallow dive in a head-on attack, F/Lt. Turner being in formation behind and to the right, close in. Both opened fire together at a height of 50 feet and speed 200 m.p.h. Saw bullets strike water ahead of E-boat and then hitting E-boat. Got one burst from front guns of E-boat - no damage. E-boat ceased fire. F/Lt. Turner, having converged slightly on me, turned away to avoid slipstream as he passed over E-boat. I continued and sprayed drifter 200 yards behind E-boat. One burst from the drifter before I opened fire and none as my bullets struck drifter. Passed over the drifter and made for home with F/Lt. Turner in formation. Did not stop to observe damage to boats, but E-boat must have had a lot as we could see bullets from 16 guns hitting the boat; drifter probably did not receive so much damage - probably killed a few of the crew. Returned home and landed at 1135 hrs.

Weather ideal for mosquito raid.

                                     Signed: D.R.S. Bader S/Ldr.
                                                 D.S.O. D.F.C.

                                     Flight: A.
                                     Squadron: 242.

Patrol No. 2. 1215-1315 hrs.

I was airborne from Martlesham at 12.15, flying No. 2 to F/O McKnight, D.F.C. together with F/O Tamblyn, D.F.C. and F/O Rogers as second pair. We set out for the French coast, crossing the English coast off Felixstowe and eventually sighted the French coast to the east of Dyck Lightship. Here we split from F/O Tamblyn and F/O Rogers and F/O McKnight and I turned down coast. When just past Dyck Lightship we sighted an "E" boat upon which we both made two attacks, seeing our fire boat upon which we both made two attacks, seeing our fire hitting its deck. Following upon our low level attacks, both from astern, the "E" boat made immediately for shore. We then turned back up coast leaving Dyck Lightship on our port and crossed the French coast just west of Gravelines where we sighted practically on the beach a fairly large concentration of troops, entrenched and extending fairly well inland. (A rough estimate would be 1 mile deep but it is very hard to give an exact estimate). The entrenchments also had the appearance

PUBLIC RECORD OFFICE

PRIME MINISTER'S
PERSONAL TELEGRAM   90
SERIAL No. T 687

MOST SECRET

FOR THE FORMER NAVAL PERSON FROM THE PRESIDENT

The outcome of the Moscow Conference delighted me. Getting the goods to them is the important thing now. I learn from Admiral Stark that the difficult problem which yesterday I presented to you is being solved. I appreciate your cooperation in reaching the solution. I am looking forward to seeing Attlee.

Scrambled Chequers
11.40 pm   10/10 Starkey

Winston Churchill and Franklin D. Roosevelt had a close personal relationship which led to an almost daily series of telegrams between the two men. This telegram was sent by Roosevelt to Churchill and reports on the decision to send supplies to Russia, by convoy, in 1941.
Public Record Office, PREM 3/469

Their Finest Hour

During most of the 1930s the British government, largely supported by its citizens, had pursued a policy of appeasement towards Nazi Germany. This had led to the dismemberment of Czechoslovakia at Munich in October 1938. British policy changed when it became clear that Hitler could not be contained. When the Germans attacked Poland on 1 September 1939, the British Government sent this ultimatum demanding that the Germans withdrew or face war with Britain and France. The document was ignored by the Germans.

British Library, Additional MS. 56401, f. 161

Minutes of a Cabinet meeting held on 22 July 1940 which discussed German peace overtures, but took the momentous decision to fight on alone.

Public Record Office, CAB 65/8 209(40)11

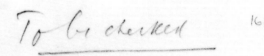

To be checked 161

---

137   W.M. 209 (40).

showed great prevision in suggesting that Hitler was likely to start a peace offensive at an early date.

The War Cabinet took note of these telegrams.

Discussion then ensued on a suggestion that Resolutions should be put down for debate in both Houses on the following Thursday, expressing the resolve of this country to fight on until nazism had been defeated. These Resolutions might be proposed and seconded by Private Members in the Commons, and by Peers who held no Government post in the Lords. After a short and rather formal Debate a free vote should be allowed.

In favour of this course it was argued that it would be undesirable that the occasion of Herr Hitler's speech should be allowed to pass without any notice being taken of it. The procedure of Resolutions in both Houses would show the strength of our institutions, and would serve to associate the whole country with the Government's determination and resolve.

Against this, it was said that public morale in the country was so good that no formal expression of it was necessary at the present time. The procedure of Resolutions in both Houses was not one which could be used frequently and there was much to be said for keeping it for some later occasion.

The view was also expressed that Herr Hitler's speech was intended for home consumption. It did not contain any specific offer, the rejection of which would call for immediate action on Hitler's part, but made an appeal which did not call for any definite reply.

The War Cabinet—
Invited the Prime Minister to discuss this suggestion with the Parliamentary Secretary to the Treasury.

Defence Regulation 18B.
Custody of persons detained.
(Previous Reference: W.M. (40) 183rd Conclusions, Minute 10.)

12. The War Cabinet had before them a Memorandum by the Home Secretary dealing with the question whether it would be desirable to transfer overseas 600 members of the British Union of Fascists who had been detained under Defence Regulation 18B (W.P. (40) 273). *The Home Secretary* said that it was very doubtful whether there was any suitable place in the Colonies to which these people could be sent. Before any persons detained under the Defence Regulations could be sent to a self-governing Dominion, amending legislation would be necessary. He thought that such legislation would be controversial.

In discussion, the view was expressed that all the accommodation which could be made available in the Dominions or Colonies would be required for interned aliens, for prisoners of war, or for special classes, *e.g.*, the Gibraltarians who had been evacuated from Gibraltar. In these circumstances there was much to be said for keeping the 600 members of the British Union of Fascists in this country, under suitable conditions.

The War Cabinet—
Decided not to proceed further at the present time with the suggestion to transfer overseas the members of the British Union of Fascists who had been detained under Defence Regulation 18B.

On the instructions of H.M. Principal Secretary of State for Foreign Affairs, I have the honour to make the following communication.

Early this morning the German Chancellor issued a proclamation to the German Army which indicated clearly that he was about to attack Poland.

At   this morning the German Chancellor issued

Information which has reached His Majesty's Government in the United Kingdom and the French Government indicates that German troops have crossed the Polish frontier and that attacks upon Polish towns are proceeding.

If this information is correct it appears to the Government of the United Kingdom and France that by their action the German Government have created conditions (viz. an aggressive act of force against Poland threatening the independence of Poland) which call for the implementation by the Governments of the United Kingdom and France of the undertaking to Poland to come to her assistance.

I am accordingly to inform Your Excellency that unless the German Government can immediately satisfy His Majesty's Government in the United Kingdom that these reports are unfounded, or in the alternative are prepared to give His Majesty's Government satisfactory assurances that the German Government has suspended all aggressive action against Poland and are prepared promptly to withdraw their forces from Polish territory, His Majesty's Government in the United Kingdom will without hesitation fulfil their obligations to Poland.

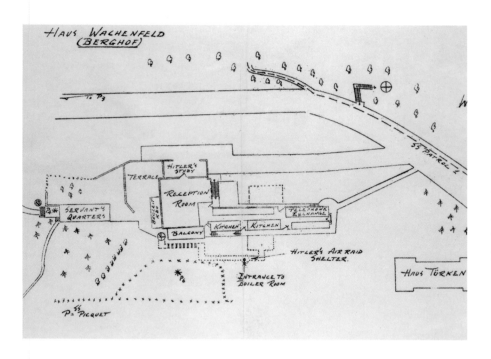

The tide eventually turned in the Allies' favour in late 1942: the result of American economic and military strength and the might of the Russian Red Army. British forces fought across three continents. Tens of thousands of aircraft and tanks were turned out by factories across the United Kingdom. British scientists developed some of the most important inventions of the war. And British support for resistance movements in Occupied Europe helped considerably to keep Nazi forces tied down. But at the end of the war much of the world was ravaged and severe economic and political dislocation followed.

Plan of Haus Wachenfeld, Berchtesgarten near Salzburg which was Adolf Hitler's Alpine retreat. One of the most remarkable secrets of the war recently revealed was the British plan to assassinate Hitler. There were months of detailed preparation before the idea was abandoned in October 1944. It was noted on the file: 'As a strategist Hitler has been of the greatest possible assistance to the British war effort'.
Public Record Office, HS 6/624 f17

Five x-rays were taken of Hitler's head by his physician Dr Giessing on 19 September 1944 while Giessing was trying to cure Hitler of persistent ear ache caused by the attempt on his life on 20 July. The x-rays were used in a British Army report of 1946 on Hitler's death.
Public Record Office, WO 208/3789

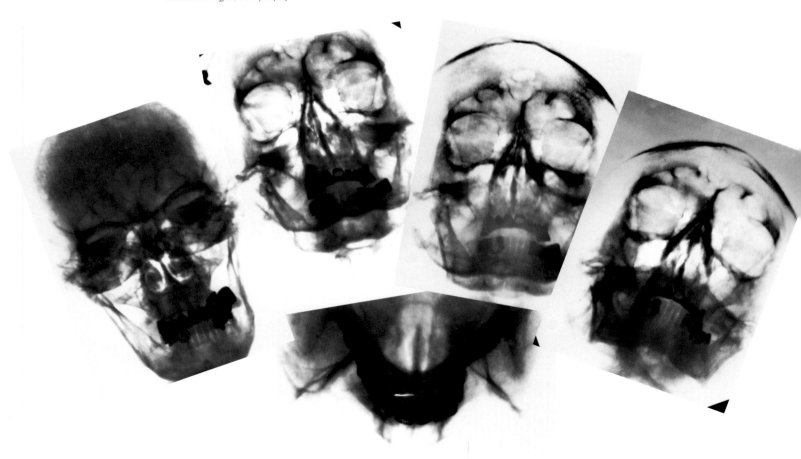

The Turn of the Tide

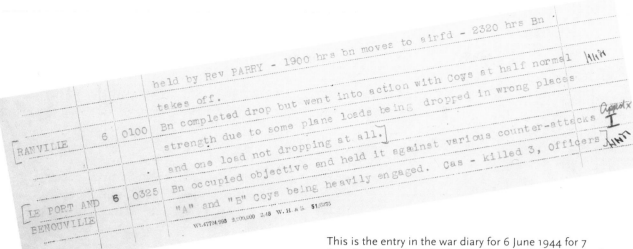

held by Rev PARRY - 1900 hrs bn moves to airfd - 2320 hrs Bn takes off.

RANVILLE   6   0100   Bn completed drop but went into action with Coys at half normal strength due to some plane loads being dropped in wrong places and one load not dropping at all.]

LE PORT AND   6   0325   Bn occupied objective and held it against various counter-attacks
BENOUVILLE   "A" and "B" Coys being heavily engaged. Cas - killed 3, Officers

This is the entry in the war diary for 6 June 1944 for 7 Battalion, Parachute Regiment. The Battalion were the first British airborne troops to land, just after midnight, on D-Day near Ranville in Normandy. They destroyed vital bridges behind beaches where allied troops were due to land later in the day.
Public Record Office, WO 171/1239

The poster was drawn by an unknown artist probably for use in Australia or south east Asia. The fall of Singapore in February 1942 had been a major blow to British prestige in the region. The poster may have been commissioned by the Ministry of Information to remind people that the British and their Australian allies were still fighting the Japanese in the jungles of Burma and New Guinea.
Public Record Office, INF 3/1350

Work in factories was a fruitful source of inspiration for war artists, as this drawing by Rowland Hilder for the Ministry of Information shows. The British economy was largely turned over to war work. Women, as well as men, were conscripted and directed to work in factories such as this one building planes for the RAF.
Public Record Office, INF 3/803

The term 'Welfare State' is usually associated with initiatives of the late 1940s, and particularly the establishment of the National Health Service in 1947. But these developments rested on reforms introduced by governments of all political colours throughout the 20th century. Concerns about the poor health of young men recruited for the South African (Boer) War led to demands for the provision of school meals, and in 1906 legislation was passed to enable local authorities to provide such meals. Medical examination of school children was introduced the following year. A non-contributory old-age pension scheme was introduced in 1908, and in his 1909 'People's Budget', Lloyd George set out the Liberal Party's proposals for tackling unemployment through

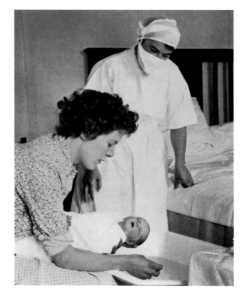

voluntary labour exchanges, a limited scheme of unemployment insurance, and plans to reduce the severity of trade fluctuations. Minimum wage legislation was introduced the same year, and extended in 1912. Health insurance introduced in 1911 made provision for sanatoria and for expenditure on medical research, and in 1914 grants were given to local authorities for nursing and clinical services.

During the First World War the health of mothers and small children was particularly emphasised in a well-publicised argument that high infant mortality made it more dangerous to be a baby than a soldier. Local authorities were encouraged to improve their services, and the government provided funding for ante-natal and child-care clinics, home visitors, hospital treatment and food for mothers and children in need. The inter-war years saw some advance

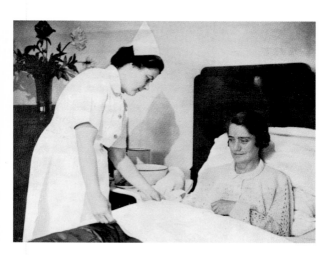

As part of a campaign to ensure that people knew what was available to them under the new National Health Service, local authorities produced publicity material for their services, from which these illustrations are taken.
Public Record Office, MH 134/6

along the road to a Welfare State; for example old-age and survivor's insurance was introduced in 1925. But in a period which saw slump and depression there was a natural reluctance to extend reform.

The Second World War saw the establishment of the Emergency Medical Service, and some welfare schemes such as unemployment assistance were amended, but other projected welfare reforms and initiatives, such as the raising of the school leaving age and an investigation into workman's compensation, were abandoned. Churchill was personally hostile to social reform, and, in particular, opposed anything which detracted from the immediate waging of the war – a view shared by the Treasury. But during the same period there was considerable activity at a lower political and administrative level, and many official enquiries, such as that of the Beveridge Committee, were instituted which were to provide the consensus of expert advice on which later reconstruction plans were based. The post-war Labour government was able to build on this

groundwork not only in establishing the National Health Service but also in extending social security provision, reforming educational provision in line with the 1944 Butler Act, and introducing legislation to form the basis of post-war town and country planning.

Indian Independence

India had been the jewel in the crown of the British Empire, but demands for self-rule had began as early as the 1870s, and the Indian National Congress was formed in 1885. During the First World War, the home rule movement gained great momentum, and in 1919 British authority in India was undermined following the slaughter by the British army of 379 unarmed Indian demonstrators at Amritsar. Mohandas, later known as 'Mahatma', Gandhi, a lawyer, emerged as the leader of the Indian nationalist movement. Gandhi urged a policy of non-violent passive resistance to British rule. The British government attempted to defuse the nationalist movement by offering constitutional reform, but the result was political deadlock. Following the Second World War, the new Labour government in Britain accepted the need for independence, but the question of whether Muslim areas should form a separate country took India to the verge of civil war. At midnight on 14–15 August 1947, India and Pakistan became independent and separate states, but there was immediately an outbreak of religious violence, in which 250,000 people lost their lives and over 5.5 million refugees left their homes.

In 1942, a British mission had offered India dominion status, but this was rejected by Gandhi and the Congress party. The 73-year old Gandhi was imprisoned, and started a 21-day penitential fast. Concerned about Gandhi's health, the British offered to release him temporarily, but, in this letter (above) of 8 February 1943 to Sir Richard Tottenham, the Secretary of State for the Home Department, Gandhi refused the offer. Ten days later, Tottenham sent a memorandum to the Viceroy advising him of the code word that would be used if Gandhi died. Gandhi survived the fast, but in 1944 his health deteriorated further, and he was released from jail.

British Library, India Office Records, R/3/1/298

The final personal report of the last Viceroy of India, Lord Mountbatten of Burma, made on 16 August 1947, immediately after the end of British rule in India.

British Library, India Office Records, L/PO/6/123, f. 245

For more than four decades after the end of the Second World War, until the fall of the Berlin Wall in 1989, the two superpowers, the United States and Soviet Union, were locked in a military and ideological conflict known as the Cold War. Mutual nuclear deterrence was the key to their fragile co-existence, punctuated by periodic crises and savage conflicts across the world. Throughout this time Britain largely remained a loyal ally of the United States both in Europe and elsewhere, particularly Asia where British influence remained strong.

A mushroom cloud resulting from the explosion of a British atomic weapon on the Monte Bello Islands off the coast of Western Australia in 1952. These experiments were conducted in great secrecy. To many politicians Britain's possession of nuclear weapons represented the country's continued status as a great power.
Public Record Office, AIR 8/2309

TOP SECRET   7

effective in the circumstances of 1970, or depending heavily on American techniques. No fourth or subsequent nuclear Power is likely to be able on its own by 1970 to dispose of anything approaching the nuclear power even of the United Kingdom but changes in American policy might lead to the development of a NATO strategic nuclear force.

27. It is difficult to predict how many other individual nuclear Powers will emerge. (In this context a nuclear Power is defined as a country with nuclear weapons whose use is not subject to an external veto.) Nothing is likely to prevent France, either alone or with United States and United Kingdom co-operation, from developing some nuclear capacity. Other countries which could do so alone include West Germany, Sweden, China, East Germany, Czechoslovakia, Canada, India, Japan and just possibly the Argentine, Brazil and Israel. But in most cases the weapons would be crude and without any effective means of delivery.

28. Whether these countries will do so is another matter. An effective test suspension agreement would be a powerful deterrent (though it is quite possible to make a crude but effective untested weapon). But if the existing nuclear Powers can be persuaded to pass on tested designs or " know-how ", the suspension of tests will not prevent the emergence of at least some new nuclear Powers. It seems probable that if one side does this, the other may follow suit. Much also depends on the attitude of France. If she goes ahead with West European integration, her nuclear capacity may in effect merge into a " European " deterrent under joint control. But if she relapses into isolation, the West Germans are likely to press for their own nuclear weapons, and Russia's allies will probably do the same. Other than France, only China of the countries listed above has indicated any clear intention of manufacturing nuclear weapons. With a determined effort China could probably do so towards the middle of the decade.

(B) THE UNCOMMITTED AND BACKWARD COUNTRIES

29. On the assumption that there is no general war and no major Russian advance in Europe, the main struggle will be for influence and power in the countries outside Europe. They vary immensely. But certain features are almost universal.

(a) Most of the uncommitted countries and some of our allies are waiting to see which side wins. They will die in no last ditches. They have little or no ingrained attachment either to Marxist or, with certain exceptions (e.g., India and Israel), to Western liberal ideas.

(b) Nearly all of them are in urgent need of capital for economic development and they will accept it from any quarter without regard to political alignments. While Western generosity will probably not by itself win new friends for the Western camp, the lack of it may cause additions to the ranks of our enemies.

(c) The gap between the advanced countries of the West and the Soviet bloc, on the one hand, and the under-developed countries of Asia and Africa on the other will widen. This is not likely to be conducive to international political stability.

(d) The dominant political motive will continue to be national independence, and great advantage will accrue in the next 10 years to the side which successfully represents itself as its champion. This will cut both ways. Colonial Powers which appear to be clinging to their remaining possessions, or which fail to solve their multi-racial problems, will suffer; but if this can be avoided, the growing awareness of peoples and Governments that Sino-Soviet imperialism is the real threat to their independence should tell on our side.

(e) The trend away from parliamentary government is likely to continue.

Africa

30. The division between North and Tropical Africa will remain. In North Africa events will chiefly depend upon the outcome of the Algerian War. If no solution emerges, there will be a risk that rabid nationalism fomented from Russia will pose a grave threat to the southern flank of NATO.

31. South of the Sahara, territories which are now colonies will have obtained their independence, but are likely to remain separate States rather than to form closer associations, pressure for greater unity being frustrated by local rivalries.

TOP SECRET

During 1959 the British Prime Minister, Harold Macmillan, set up a committee to consider various strategic questions likely to affect Britain during the decade ahead. The committee foresaw that the tensions between the Soviet Union and the West would continue throughout the 1960s, but was less sure if Britain's future lay with the Commonwealth or in Europe.
Public Record Office, CAB 134/1929 f36

YEH CHIEN-YU: *Statue of Liberty*

Communist Chinese cartoon taken from *The Paper Tiger: a Collection of Anglo-American Cartoons* published in Peking in 1951. This one by Yeh Cheigu of the Statute of Liberty is subtitled 'It now has nothing to do with the ideals of the American people: it represents the Wall Street profiteers.' These crude but effective cartoons impressed Foreign Office officials with their potential as propaganda.
Public Record Office, FO 370/2231 LR22/103

George Orwell

George Orwell, the pseudonym of Eric Blair (1903–50), is remembered as the author of the vivid anti-totalitarian fables *Animal Farm* (1945) and *Nineteen Eighty-Four* (1949). However, many critics consider that his finest work is found in the various essays and journalism produced by him in the 1930s and 1940s. These explore many of the key themes of English life and national identity in the 20th century. In *Shooting An Elephant*, Orwell reflects on the nature of imperial authority, while in *Politics and the English Language* he examines the way in which language is manipulated for political ends. Other essays focus on characteristic features of English popular culture: *The Art of Donald McGill* (seaside postcards); *Boy's Weeklies*; *Such, Such were the Joys* (prep schools); *The Moon under Water* (pubs); and *The Sporting Spirit* (the cult of the 'good sport'). Orwell's descriptions of the privations of the English poor and working classes in *The Road to Wigan Pier* (1937) and elsewhere are harrowing. *The Lion and the Unicorn* (1940) is one of the best descriptions of English life, but Orwell's vision is a questioning, challenging one: 'The clatter of clogs in the Lancashire mill towns, the to-and-fro of the lorries on the Great North Road, the queues outside the Labour Exchanges, the rattle of pin-tables in the Soho pubs, the old maids biking to Holy Communion through the mists of the autumn morning – all these are not only fragments, but *characteristic* fragments, of the English scene. How can one make a pattern of this muddle?'. One of the main reasons for Orwell's power as a writer was his ability to make sense of the muddle and perceive the wider truth lurking in such personal experiences and impressions.

Animal Farm and *Ninety Eighty-Four* were hugely influential among dissident movements in the Soviet bloc during the Cold War. Translations were passed around in unofficial typed or handwritten copies, even though the penalty for possession of Orwell's works could be a prison sentence. Orwell's books influenced the *Solidarity* movement in Poland and thus helped contribute to the collapse of Soviet rule. This is the cover of a 1954 Latvian translation of *Animal Farm*.
British Library, X.958/22378

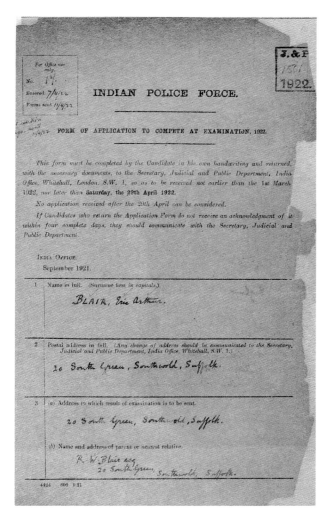

Orwell served in the Burma police from 1922–7. These are his application papers to join the police. Orwell's Burmese experiences inspired his first novel, *Burmese Days* (1934), and his essay *Shooting an Elephant*, describing an incident in which an elephant went on the rampage and Orwell had to shoot it: 'And it was at this moment, as I stood there with the rifle in my hands, that I first grasped the hollowness, the futility of the white man's dominion in the East. Here was I, the white man with his gun, standing in front of the unarmed native crowd – seemingly the leading actor of the piece; but in reality I was only an absurd puppet pushed to and fro by the will of those yellow faces behind'.
British Library, India Office Library and Records, L/PJ/6/1827

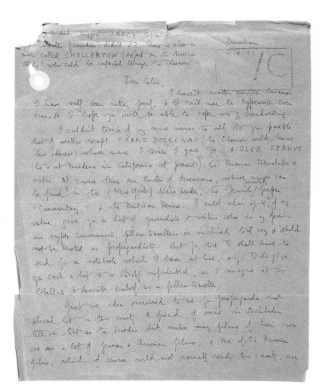

Orwell's concerns about the dangers of totalitarian rule in the late 1940s was such that in 1949 he wrote to a friend in the Foreign Office offering to provide 'a list of journalists & writers who in my opinion are crypto-communists, fellow-travellers or inclined that way & should not be trusted as propagandists'.
Public Record Office, FO 1110/189

Britain Celebrates: the Festival of Britain and the Coronation

The Festival of Britain in 1951 marked an explicit attempt by the Labour government to reward the British people for the dreariness of post-war rationing and austerity and, by casting it aside, to bring fun and colour into their lives. The serious themes underpinning the Great Exhibition of 1851 — art and science, knowledge and development — were revisited, but the style was deliberately clean and new, modern and light, and the tone witty and whimsical, as exemplified by the Skylon. At the heart of the Festival site on the South Bank in London was the Royal Festival Hall, which still survives as one of London's greatest buildings, and the more ephemeral Dome of Discovery, a pavilion celebrating the achievements of science.

This panorama of the Festival site — standing out against the dark London landscape — is an original watercolour by J. Fraser, preserved in the Festival of Britain archive.
    From right to left, the significant buildings are the Dome of Discovery, the Skylon and the Royal Festival Hall. The artist has contrasted the brightness and modernity of these structures with the grim background of post-war London.
Public Record Office, Work 25/64/gen/24

With Loyal Greetings from the National Savings Movement

A souvenir of the Coronation of Her Majesty Queen Elizabeth II

THE CORONATION REGALIA

The Coronation of Queen Elizabeth II took place on 2 June 1953, the thirty-eighth to be celebrated in Westminster Abbey since 1066. The ceremony and pageantry encompassed the old and new sides of Britain and her dominions: the order of service was based on the rite compiled for the coronation of King Edgar at Bath in 973; much of the symbolism was imperial, with attendees representing all parts of Britain's empire; but it was also a special event for the British people which bolstered a sense of national community. A key element in this was the BBC's broadcast of it, watched by millions of people. Richard Dimbleby's commentary was imbued with the notion of royalty as an embodiment of Britain's greatness.

In 1940, George Orwell wrote: 'The place to look for the germs of the future England is in light-industry areas and along the arterial roads…It is a rather restless, cultureless life, centring around tinned food, *Picture Post,* the radio and the internal combustion engine. It is a civilisation in which children grow up with an intimate knowledge of magnetoes and in complete ignorance of the Bible. To that civilisation belong the people who are most at home in and most definitely *of* the modern world, the technicians and the higher-paid skilled workers, the airmen and the mechanics, the radio experts, film producers, popular journalists and industrial chemists.' The heroes of this new England included inventors and scientists such as Frank Whittle, John Logie Baird and Alexander Fleming, whose inventions and discoveries are fundamental to modern life.

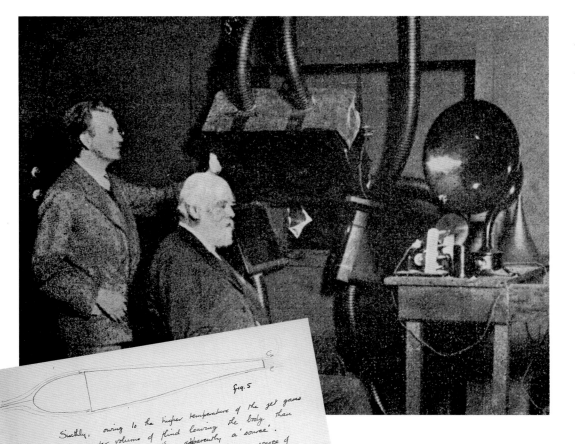

The Scottish electrical engineer John Logie Baird (1888–1946) was forced to take early retirement as a result of bad health and went to live in Hastings, where he conducted experiments into ways of transmitting pictures by radio. Although other scientists were working in this field, in 1926 Baird was the first to hold a successful public demonstration of a primitive televsion system. He was also the first to transmit pictures of objects in motion and developed 'noctovision', which used infra-red rays to communicate pictures from a darkened room. He is shown here (on the left) demonstrating his 'noctovision' apparatus to the British physicist and psychic researcher, Sir Oliver Lodge. Baird's mechanical system was used by the BBC for its first television broadcasts in 1929, but was soon superseded by the modern cathode ray system. In 1936, the BBC launched the world's first regular television service from its studios at Alexandra Palace.
British Library 08756.d.28

Sir Frank Whittle (1907–96) joined the Royal Air Force as a boy apprentice and became interested in jet propulsion of aircraft while attending the RAF College in Cranwell. He filed his first patent for a turbojet engine in 1930, but did not receive official backing for his work and in 1936 formed a private company for the development of his engine. This first powered flight using Whittle's engine took place on a British experimental fighter plane in May 1941 and by the end of the war jet fighters were being used by the RAF. This is one of Whittle's working notebooks.
Public Record Office, AIR 62/3, ff. 355–6

The White Heat of Technology

In 1928, the Scottish doctor and medical researcher Sir Alexander Fleming (1881–1955), in the course of his researches into influenza, noticed that a green mould growing in a culture dish at the hospital where he was working had killed the surrounding bacteria. This is a model of that original culture dish from Fleming's papers. Fleming showed in laboratory experiments that this mould, *Penicillium notatum*, was effective against many disease-causing bacteria such as those responsible for gonorrhoea and meningitis. It was not, however, until the Second World War that Fleming's experients were followed up in earnest, and Sir Howard Florey worked out a method for the industrial production of penicillin. With British factories affected by the war, Florey was forced to take his method to the United States, where the drug was put into production and helped to save the lives of many wounded servicemen.

British Library, Additional MS. 56209

In 1936, the British mathematician Alan Turing (1912–54) published a paper 'On Computable Numbers' which described a theoretical computing device now known as a Turing machine. This concept was fundamental in the development of the digital computer. During the Second World War, Turing played a leading role in the deciphering of German military signals at Bletchley Park in Buckinghamshire. He urged the use of computing machines to help crack German codes. In 1943, the Bletchley Park team built Colossus, shown here, one of the first of all electronic digital computers. It incorporated 1,500 vacuum tubes.

Public Record Office, FO 850/234

Despite Ireland's successful challenge to empire, and the growing credibility of the independence movement in India, Britain's confidence in the enduring nature of her colonial empire remained largely intact until the end of the Second World War. Then, pressure from her allies and rapidly developing nationalist feeling within the colonies combined to demand a reassessment of policy. In 1941, at their Atlantic meeting, Roosevelt and Churchill had expressed their respect for 'the rights of all peoples to choose the form of government under which they live'. Although it was subsequently argued that they had in mind those European countries occupied by Germany, the implications for the colonies were obvious.

In 1948, the Colonial Secretary stressed that the fundamental aim of British colonial policy was to guide the colonies to responsible self-government in conditions ensuring a fair standard of living, and freedom from oppression, for all their peoples – a formulation derived from high-level policy discussion in the context of India, Burma and Ceylon, all of which achieved independence in 1947–48. No formal time-scale was set out, however, and the British government showed itself prepared to resist forcibly any development which it considered undesirable, such as the so-called 'Mau Mau' rebellion in Kenya and communist insurgency in Malaya. Indeed, by the late 1940s Britain's American allies considered communism to be a much greater danger than residual colonialism. In 1956 the policy of steady development intended to lead gradually to autonomy was dealt a blow by the politically disastrous attack on Egypt launched by Britain and France. Although the Gold Coast achieved its independence, as Ghana, the following year as part of the planned and gradual process, by 1960 Harold Macmillan, in his famous 'winds of change' speech to the Cape Parliament, signalled an altogether more rapid dissolution of Empire.

African school children study under a wall map of their continent showing British colonies traditionally marked 'red on the map' – an image soon to be swept away.
Public Record Office, INF 13/230 (no. 4)

On 3 February 1960, as the culmination of his tour of Africa, Harold Macmillan addressed both houses of the Parliament of the Union of South Africa in Cape Town. The speech attracted enormous publicity, primarily because of Macmillan's frank statement that some aspects of South African policy made it impossible for Britain to give South Africa her support and encouragement without being 'false to our own deep convictions about the political destinies of free men ...'
Public Record Office, CO 859/1477 (no. 5)

MEMORANDUM

Minister for External Affairs intends to visit Ghana later this year. All this proves your determination, as the most advanced industrial country of the continent, to play your part in the new Africa of today.

Sir, as I have travelled round the Union I have found everywhere, as I expected, a deep preoccupation with what is happening in the rest of the African continent. I understand and sympathise with your interest in these events, and your anxiety about them. Ever since the break up of the Roman Empire one of the constant facts of political life in Europe has been the emergence of independent nations. They have come into existence over the centuries in different forms, with different kinds of Government, but all have been inspired by a deep, keen feeling of nationalism which has grown as the nations have grown.

In the twentieth century and especially since the end of the war, the processes which gave birth to the nation states of Europe have been repeated all over the world. We have seen the awakening of national consciousness in peoples who have for centuries lived in dependence upon some other power. Fifteen years ago this movement spread through Asia. Many countries there of different races and civilisations pressed their claim to an independent national life. Today the same thing is happening in Africa and the most striking of all the impressions I have formed since I left London a month ago is of the strength of this African national consciousness. In different places it takes different forms but it is happening everywhere. The wind of change is blowing through this continent and, whether we like it or not,

/this

The End of Empire

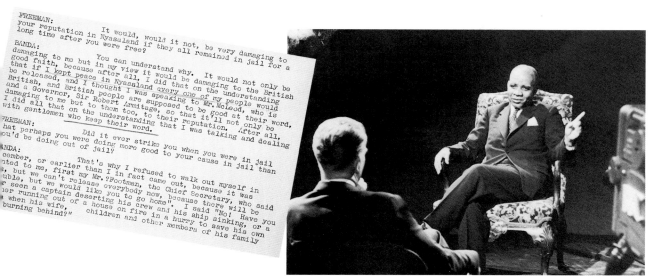

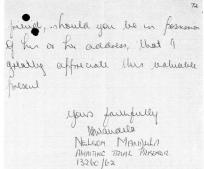

Like many other nationalist leaders, Dr Hastings Banda of Nyasaland (later Malawi) was imprisoned by the British. Shortly after his release in April 1960 he was interviewed by John Freeman for BBC-TV.

Public Record Office, CO 1015/2439 (no. 94)

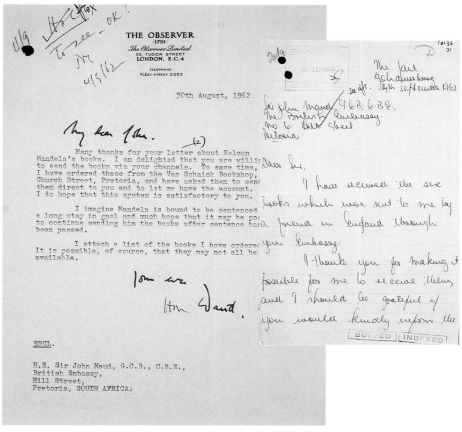

(above and above right) In August 1962, David Astor, editor of the *Observer*, wrote to the British High Commissioner in South Africa asking about 'the possibility of getting books sent to a man in gaol'. The man was Nelson Mandela, awaiting trial in Johannesburg. The books which Astor subsequently sent included Theodore H. White's *The Making of the President*.

Public Record Office, DO 119/1478

(right) Writing in April 1957 some weeks after Ghana attained independence, Prime Minister Kwame Nkrumah thanked Macmillan for sending a high-level delegation to the celebrations, and expressed his hopes for a 'continuing happy association' with Britain.

Public Record Office, PREM 11/1859 f.17

In 1917, the prime ministers of the Dominions, meeting in London as members of Lloyd George's War Cabinet, called for a readjustment of constitutional relations, which 'should be based upon a full recognition of the dominions as autonomous nations of an Imperial Commonwealth and of India as an important portion of the same, should recognise the right of the Dominions and India to an adequate voice in foreign policy … and should provide effective arrangements for continuous consultation on all important matters of common Imperial concern'. In 1926 the Balfour Declaration defined the constitutional relationship between Great Britain and the dominions as 'autonomous communities within the British Empire, equal in status, in no way subordinate one to another', although it was not until 1931 that the Statute of Westminster clarified the legal position of the dominions parliaments.

India's wish to join the Commonwealth and also to become a republic was accommodated by altering the requirement for allegiance to the Crown to a declaration that the British sovereign was recognised as 'Head of the Commonwealth'. The Irish Republic, on the other hand, chose to leave the Commonwealth. Subsequently, most colonies applied for membership as they achieved independence. Burma never joined; others such as Pakistan and South Africa have had breaks in their membership. In 1995 Mozambique became the first member with no previous formal link with the British Empire and Commonwealth. In 1965 the Commonwealth established its own independent and international Secretariat, at Marlborough House in London.

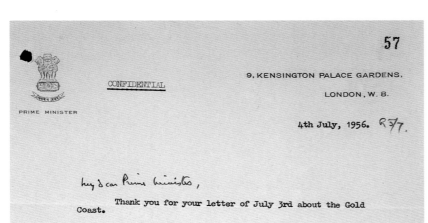

The admittance of new members to the Commonwealth is agreed by existing members. Such consent was given in advance of Ghana's independence. In this letter to the British Prime Minister Anthony Eden the Indian President Nehru expressed his country's enthusiastic support of Ghana's admittance. Not all members were as happy with the proposal as India.
Public Record Office, PREM 11/1367, f. 57

Jomo Kenyatta, Prime Minister of Kenya, in London for the Commonwealth Prime Ministers Conference of 1964.
Public Record Office, MEPO 2/10633

Britain in Europe

The first post-war British call for European unity was made by Churchill in Zurich in 1946. His chief concern was to prevent further conflict between France and Germany, and he did not envisage that Britain, in whose independent greatness he ardently believed, should become formally part of a united Europe. Churchill's view was shared by Ernest Bevin, the Labour Government's Foreign Secretary from 1945 to 1951, with the result that Britain played no part in the initial attempts to achieve continental co-operation such as the establishment of the European Coal and Steel Community. By the time the Treaty of Rome was signed in 1957, many believed that Britain should play some role in Europe, but the British government was unwilling to join a customs union maintaining a common tariff against the rest of the world. By 1961 the Prime Minister, Harold Macmillan, and most of his party, had become convinced that Britain should apply for full membership. This alarmed members of the Commonwealth, not primarily for reasons of sentiment, but because of Britain's importance as a market for their agricultural products. However, in 1963 General de Gaulle brutally vetoed Britain's application to join the Common Market. Harold Wilson sought to lead the Labour government in the same direction – away from Empire and the United States, and towards Europe – but with no more success, and so it fell to Edward Heath to carry Britain into Europe in 1972.

On 14 January 1963 General de Gaulle spelt out his objections to British membership of the Common Market at a press conference at the Elysee Palace in Paris. De Gaulle stressed that the protection of agriculture was of prime importance for the Common Market, and declared that England was an island maritime country, with trade and markets in many diverse countries, and an economy based primarily on manufacturing and commerce, not agriculture. The distinctive and marked traditions of all aspects of English economic life made it impossible, in De Gaulle's view, for England readily to be integrated into the Common Market.
Public Record Office, FO 371/169114 CF1022/5

On 22 January 1972, a decade after Britain's first application to join the EEC, the then Prime Minister Edward Heath, together with the Foreign Secretary Alec Douglas-Home and Minister for Europe Geoffrey Rippon, signed this treaty, by which the United Kingdom was formally admitted to membership of the EEC effective from the beginning of 1973.
Public Record Office, FO 949/146

Nationalist movements in 19th-century America, Europe and elsewhere found an echo in Britain. Encouraged by Irish demands for home rule, campaigns began to secure greater independence for Scotland and Wales. In Wales, the Welsh language provided a special focus of national sentiment. The ancient music and literary festivals known as *eisteddfodau* were revived in the 18th century in the form of local tavern events organised by leading literary figures. From the beginning of the 19th century, *eisteddfodau* became the chief vehicle of Welsh cultural life. It was about this time that *Gorsedd Beirdd Ynys Prydain* (Assembly of Bards of the Island of Britain), an institution which became linked with the *eisteddfod*, was invented by Edward Williams ('Iolo Morganwg'), in an attempt to recreate Druidic traditions. The movement to establish a national *eisteddfod* for Wales gained impetus throughout the 19th century and a National Eisteddfod Society was formed in the 1860s to arrange the annual event. From 1870, growing demands for greater Welsh autonomy led to the establishment of such national institutions as the University of Wales, the National Library of Wales and the National Museum as well as the creation of a Welsh Office and the

Water-colour drawing, 1798, by William Owen-Pughe of Edward Williams, 'Iolo Morganwg' (1747–1826), the inventor of the Gorsedd of Bards.
National Library of Wales

disestablishment of the Welsh Church. Nevertheless, the first half of the 20th century saw a decline in the number of Welsh-speakers. The Welsh nationalist party, *Plaid Cymru*, was founded in 1925, with the aim of safeguarding Welsh-speaking communities from such threats as the drowning of valleys to create water reservoirs for English cities. From the 1960s, there have been successful campaigns to secure recognition of Welsh as a legal language and to establish a Welsh television channel, and the number of Welsh speakers is now increasing.

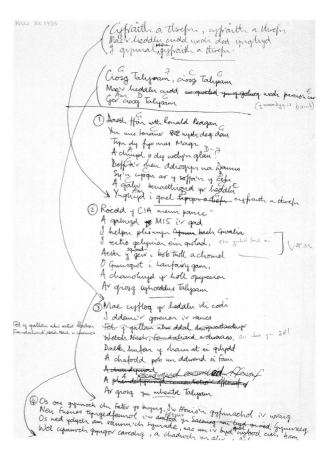

Draft of a satirical protest song, 'Ciosg Talysarn', by Dafydd Iwan who is well-known in Wales for his patriotic songs. This particular song, dating from 1982, celebrates an infamous public telephone kiosk at Tal-y-sarn, Gwynedd, which was reputedly tapped by intelligence officers during inquiries into the holiday home arson campaign.
National Library of Wales

Photograph by the newspaper photographer Geoff Charles, of a protest march, February-March 1971, from St Asaph to the BBC studios at Bangor where television licences were burnt by members of *Cymdeithas yr Iaith Gymraeg* (the Welsh Language Society), who were calling for a Welsh language television channel.
National Library of Wales

Logo of the Welsh language television channel, *Sianel Pedwar Cymru* (S4C), established in 1982, following protests by *Cymdeithas yr Iaith Gymraeg* which included a hunger strike by Dr Gwynfor Evans.

Eisteddfodau and Thistles

In Scotland, language was also, in a different way, very important in the resurgence of national feeling. The most distinctive voice of Scottish nationalism, Hugh McDiarmid (the pseudonym of Christopher Murray Grieve, 1892–1978), first came to attention with his 1926 poem *A Drunk Man Looks at the Thistle*, a book-length poem reflecting on Scotland and Scottishness which sought to realise the 'hitherto unrealised potentialities of Braid Scots' as a poetic tongue. In 1928, McDiarmid was one of the founders of the National Party of Scotland which in 1934 merged with the Scottish Party to form the Scottish National Party. McDiarmid was expelled from the SNP for his communism, but remained one of the most strident and effective advocates of Scottish nationalism, listing his recreation in *Who's Who* as 'Anglophobia'. During the 1970s, it seemed as if oil revenues might make Scottish separation from England a viable economic possibility, and there was a strong campaign for devolution, with the SNP enjoying considerable electoral success. The SNP suffered a considerable setback when devolution was narrowly rejected by a referendum in 1979, but during the 1990s it has enjoyed a resurgence. In 1998, a referendum supported the establishment of a Scottish parliament which in 1999 was revived after 292 years.

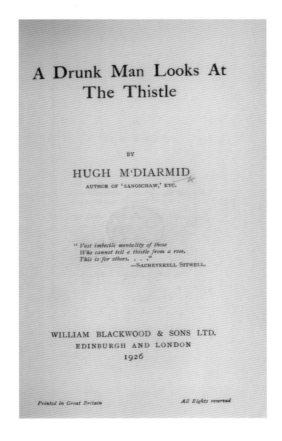

Title page of the first edition of Hugh McDiarmid's *A Drunk Man Looks at the Thistle*, published in Edinburgh in 1926.
British Library, 011645.h.45

A 1969 Limited edition of *A Drunk Man Looks at the Thistle* with illustrations by Frans Masereel.
British Library, Cup.510.ee.32.

Cartoons from 1977 editions of *The Free Scot*, the magazine of the Calderwood St Leonards branch of the Scottish National Party, referring to the attempts to secure devolution under the government of James Callaghan.
British Library, P.703/639

In 1957, Prime Minster Harold Macmillan heralded the economic recovery of Britain from post-war austerity: 'most of our people', he said, 'have never had it so good. Go round the country, ... and you will see a prosperity such as we have never had ... in [our] history'. The 'Swinging Sixties' were built on this hard won and, as it turned out, fragile prosperity and were also a reaction against it.

With new roads came new cars: the expensive, stylish and fast 'E'-type Jaguar first appeared in 1961 but from 1964 was curbed by the introduction of the 70 mph speed limit. Even this was at first regarded as potentially too great for another key British invention and style icon of the sixties, the Mini, first produced in 1959. As this government report demonstrates, officials were concerned about the dangers of excessive speed by Minis on the M4 motorway.

Public Record Office, DSIR 12/285, report no BV 534.

From the mid-1950s Britain was transformed by new high-rise buildings – stark, uncompromising monuments to modernity. The Beeching Report in 1963 recommended the closure of 20% of the rail network, while the motorway network was gradually built up from small beginnings, with the opening of the Preston by-pass in 1958 and of the first stretch of the M1 the next year. Many motorways were driven through the heart of urban areas, as this view of the Westway – the A 40 (M) – running through west London, demonstrates.

Public Record Office INF 14/181

Social attitudes were transformed in many ways, driven by the newly affluent young throwing aside respect for the culture and values of their parents. Style and fashion, too, evolved rapidly: in 1955 Mary Quant opened a new shop, Bazaar, in the King's Road, Chelsea, to sell clothes for women made to her own designs, using unconventional fabrics such as PVC and featuring trouser suits or increasingly short skirts. Within a decade the mini skirt had crept up to six inches above the knee and the King's Road, with its waif-like models, epitomised the sixties style: Biba and Habitat, also starting in the area, were among the other new businesses that were to shape the style of the future. Meanwhile Carnaby Street, off Regent Street in central London (above), had become a mecca for 'mod' fashion and the symbol of 'swinging London'.

Public Record Office, INF 14/146

Music was a key component and driver of the changes. American or American-style rock and roll and jazz had dominated the British market from the mid-fifties, but in the early sixties there emerged a style of pop music that was distinctively British. Among its exponents were the Rolling Stones, Manfred Mann and the Hollies, but most prominent of all were the Beatles who shot to fame amidst scenes of teenage hysteria in 1963. The output of the Beatles showed an increasing sophistication both of music and lyrics: this example of their work is the manuscript of the words to the classic song *Yesterday* in the handwriting of the composer, Paul McCartney.

British Library, loan 86
By kind permission Sony/ATV Music Publishing

The Falklands Factor

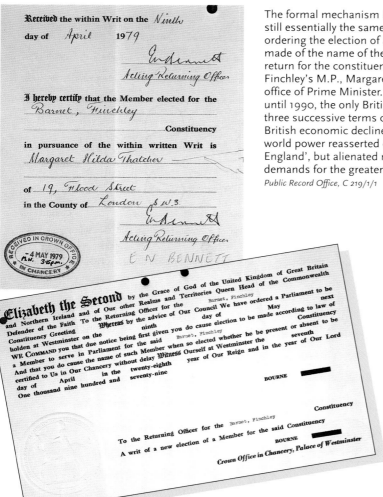

The formal mechanism by which parliamentary elections are initiated is still essentially the same as in the middle ages. Writs are sent out ordering the election of a parliamentary representative, and a return is made of the name of the member of parliament., This is the writ and return for the constituency of Finchley for the 1979 election, which saw Finchley's M.P., Margaret Thatcher, become the first woman to hold the office of Prime Minister. Margaret Thatcher served as Prime Minister until 1990, the only British political leader in the 20th century to win three successive terms of office. Her forthright views on means by which British economic decline could be reversed and Britain's authority as a world power reasserted commanded widespread support in 'middle England', but alienated many other parts of the country, fuelling demands for the greater devolution of power in Scotland and Wales.

Public Record Office, C 219/1/1

The Falklands War was a watershed in the fortunes of the Thatcher government. The jingoistic feelings encouraged by the conflict helped create support for a government which had previously been very unpopular. Britain and Spain had argued over ownership of the Falkland Islands or Islas Malvinas in the 18th century. Argentina pursued Spain's claims after it became independent, and in 1833 Britain expelled an Argentinian settlement from the Falkland Islands. In 1981, as the 150th anniversary of the expulsion approached, the military rulers of Argentina determined that the Malvinas should return to Argentinian rule. There was every reason to think that Britain would not struggle to keep control of the islands; their population was declining and the British government had been reluctant to devote any resources to their development. However, the islanders were determined to remain British subjects. In April 1982, Argentina invaded the Falklands. Britain dispatched a large military force across the South Atlantic to recapture the islands. Following some fierce engagements, with the loss of ships on both sides, the Argentian garrison capitulated on 14 June 1982.

These are the formal instruments of surrender for the Falkland Islands and the two dependencies of the Falklands also seized by the Argentinians, South Georgia and the South Sandwich Islands.

Public Record Office, DEFE 14/2

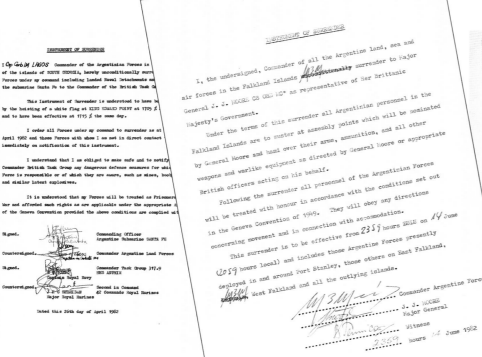

For centuries Britain's population has included immigrants, refugees and visitors from many lands. Her involvement in the Atlantic slave trade brought to England both African slaves, and African traders; black loyalists from the American wars sought refuge in London; Asian and African seamen crewed English ships and made homes in English ports; and colonials and foreigners served in the British army both at home and abroad. French Protestants fled to England from religious persecution from the 1550s onwards, and in large numbers after 1685; the Jewish community, expelled in 1290, was re-established from the mid 17th century. At an early stage in the Industrial Revolution, the internal migration of rural Englishmen and women to the industrial centres was supplemented by recruitment from Ireland. After 1945, when Irish immigration continued, increased demands for labour brought to the UK about 460,000 migrants, mainly from southern Europe, and in the years that followed the New Commonwealth became the main source of immigration. By the mid 1950s about 30,000 workers from the Caribbean, India and Pakistan were entering Britain every year. This flow continued until it was interrupted by declining economic demand and the introduction of immigration controls in the early 1960s. The final waves of immigration started in the 1970s when workers from countries such as the Philippines and Morocco came on work permits to meet demand in the service sector. Some migrants returned home, others became completely assimilated into the host community, but many others retained their distinct cultures and religions, creating the ethnic and cultural diversity of Britain's modern cities.

Black soldiers serving in British regiments in the eighteenth century included a number of musicians. Muster rolls show that William Spencer, an African, served as a kettledrummer in the Royal Horse Guards (The Blues) from at least 1759 until he died intestate in 1772. His brother-in-law's petition for Spencer's estate was discussed in Doctors Commons in 1774.
Public Record Office, T 1/508 part 2 f. 139

In the 1780s, impoverished black men, women and children in London, whose precarious existence was supplemented by charitable relief organised by the Committee for the Black Poor, were encouraged to emigrate. 675 individuals signed an agreement to travel to the west coast of Africa to establish a settlement to be known as The Land of Freedom.
Public Record Office, T1/638

Immediately after the Second World War, many West Indians who had seen war service in Britain returned in search of better career opportunities. A few years later, in June 1948, the SS Empire Windrush docked in London with the first big group of people from the Caribbean seeking employment. Although the British Government was discussing the possibility of using surplus colonial labour to meet demand, the impetus now came from the workers themselves.
Public Record Office, BT 26/1237

Further Reading and Useful Addresses

Further Reading

Benedict Anderson, *Imagined Communities: Reflections on the Origin and Spread of Nationalism* (London: Verso, 1981)

Nicolas Barker, *Treasures of the British Library* (London: The British Library, 1988)

Asa Briggs, *A Social History of England* (3rd ed., Harmondsworth: Penguin, 1999)

Iain Gordon Brown, *Building for Books: The Architectural Evolution of the Advocates' Library 1689–1925* (Aberdeen: Aberdeen University Press with National Library of Scotland, 1989)

Patrick Cadell and Ann Matheson, eds., *For the Encouragement of Learning: Scotland's National Library, 1689–1989* (Edinburgh: HMSO, 1989)

John Cantwell, *The Public Record Office 1838–1958* (London: HMSO, 1991)

Linda Colley, *Britons: Forging the Nation 1707–1837* (New Haven: Yale University Press, 1992)

John Davies, *Hanes Cymru* (Harmondsworth: Allen Lane, The Penguin Press, 1990), published in English as *The History of Wales* (Harmondsworth: Allen Lane, The Penguin Press, 1993)

G. R. Elton, *The English* (Oxford: Blackwell, 1992)

Juliet Gardiner and Neil Wenborn, eds., *The History Today Companion to British History* (London: Collins & Brown, 1995)

Dafydd Ifans, *Trysorfa Cenedl – Llyfrgell Genedlaethol Cymru* (Aberystwyth: Llyfrgell Genedlaethol Cymru, 1998), also in English as *The Nation's Heritage – The National Library of Wales* (Aberystwyth: National Library of Wales, 1998)

J. Graham Jones, *Llyfr Poced: Hanes Cymru* (Caerdydd: Gwasg Prifysgol Cymru, 1994), published in English as *A Pocket Guide: the History of Wales* (Cardiff: University of Wales Press, 1998)

Hugh Kearney, *The British Isles: A History of Four Nations* (Cambridge, Cambridge University Press, 1989)

Aidan Lawes, *Chancery Lane 1377–1977: 'The Strong Box of the Empire'* (London: Public Record Office, 1996)

Peter Marshall, ed., *The Cambridge Illustrated History of the British Empire* (Cambridge: Cambridge University Press, 1996)

Kenneth O. Morgan, ed., *The Oxford History of Britain* (Oxford and New York: Oxford University Press, 1992)

Gordon Donaldson and Robert Morpeth, *A Dictionary of Scottish History* (Edinburgh: John Donald, 1977)

Guide to the National Archives of Scotland (Edinburgh: the Stationery Office, 1996)

P. R. Harris, *A History of the British Museum Library, 1753–1973* (London: The British Library, 1998)

John and Julia Keay, eds., *Collins Encyclopaedia of Scotland* (London: HarperCollins, 1994)

Patrick Keiller, *Robinson in Space* (London: Reaktion Books, 1999)

Michael Lynch, *Scotland: a New History* (London: Barrie and Jenkins, 1991)

Andrew Prescott, *English Historical Documents* (London: The British Library, 1988)

Raphael Samuel, *Island Stories: Unravelling Britain* (*Theatres of Memory*, vol. II) (London and New York: Verso, 1998)

Useful Addresses

The British Library, 96 Euston Road, London NW1 2DB. Tel: 020 7412 7000. *Fax*: 020 7412 7787. *E-mail*: mss@bl.uk. *Web site*: www.bl.uk

Family Records Centre, 1 Myddleton Street, London EC1R 1UW. *Tel*: 020 8392 5300. *Fax*: 020 8392 5307. *E-mail*: enquiry@pro.gov.uk. *Web site*: www.pro.gov.uk

House of Lords Record Office, House of Lords, London SW1A OPW. *Tel*: 020 7219 3074. *Fax*: 020 7219 2570. *E-mail*: hlro@parliament.uk. *Web site*: www.parliament.uk

Llyfrgell Genedlaethol Cymru / National Library of Wales, Aberystwyth, Ceredigion SY23 3BU. *Tel*: 01970 632800. *Fax*: 01970 615970. *E-mail*: holi@llgc.org.uk. *Web site*: www.llgc.org.uk

National Archives of Scotland, HM General Register House, Edinburgh EH1 3YY. *Tel*: 0131 535 1314. Fax: 0131 557 9569. E-mail: research@nas.gov.uk

National Library of Scotland, George IV Bridge, Edinburgh EH1 1EW. *Tel*: 0131 226 4531. *Fax*: 0131 220 6662. *E-mail*: mss@nls.uk. *Web site*: www.nls.uk

Public Record Office, Ruskin Avenue, Kew, Richmond TW9 4DU. *Tel*: 020 7876 3444. *Fax*: (020) 7876 8905. *E-mail*: enquiry@pro.gov.uk. *Web site*: www.pro.gov.uk

Royal Commission on Historical Manuscripts, Quality House, Quality Court, Chancery Lane, London WC2A 1HP. *Tel*: (020) 7242 1198. *Fax*: (020) 7831 3550. *E-mail*: nra@hmc.gov.uk. *Web site*: www.hmc.gov.u

Index